Plato's *Republic*
Part II

Professor David Roochnik

THE TEACHING COMPANY ®

PUBLISHED BY:

THE TEACHING COMPANY
4151 Lafayette Center Drive, Suite 100
Chantilly, Virginia 20151-1232
1-800-TEACH-12
Fax—703-378-3819
www.teach12.com

ISBN 1-59803-046-9

David Roochnik, Ph.D.

Professor of Philosophy, Boston University

David Roochnik did his undergraduate work at Trinity College (Hartford, Connecticut), where he majored in philosophy. He received his Ph.D. from Pennsylvania State University in 1981.

From 1982 to 1995, Professor Roochnik taught at Iowa State University. In 1995, he moved to Boston University, where he teaches in both the Department of Philosophy and the "core curriculum," an undergraduate program in the humanities. In 1999, he won the Metcalf Prize, awarded for excellence in teaching at Boston University.

Professor Roochnik has written three books on Plato: *The Tragedy of Reason: Toward a Platonic Conception of Logos* (Routledge, 1991), *Of Art and Wisdom: Plato's Understanding of Techne* (Penn State Press, 1996), and *Beautiful City: The Dialectical Character of Plato's "Republic"* (Cornell University Press, 2003). In addition, he has published *Retrieving the Ancients: An Introduction to Greek Philosophy* (Blackwell, 2004). In 2002, he produced *An Introduction to Greek Philosophy* for The Teaching Company. He is presently working on a book on Aristotle.

Professor Roochnik is married to Gina Crandell, a professor of landscape architecture at the Rhode Island School of Design. He is the father of Lena Crandell, a freshman at Vassar College, and Shana Crandell, a sophomore at Brookline High School.

Table of Contents

Plato's *Republic*
Part II

Plato's *Republic*

Scope:

In this course, we will explore Plato's *Republic* (written in approximately 380 B.C.E.), which is the first, and arguably the most influential, work in the history of Western political philosophy. In it, Socrates, the hero of Plato's dialogue, addresses such fundamental questions as: What is justice? What is the role of education in politics? Is censorship of music and literature ever justifiable? What sort of person should rule the state? Is it ever permissible for a ruler to lie to the citizens? Should citizens be allowed full freedom when it comes to sexual relationships and private property? Are all citizens equal before the law? Should women be given the same political opportunities as men? Should everyone have equal access to health care? Socrates's answers to these and other questions will occasionally be shocking to modern ears, but they will always be thought-provoking.

The *Republic* consists of 10 "books" (or chapters), and it is divided into 4 parts. Book I is a prologue that introduces the cast of characters, of whom Socrates is far and away the most important. It also raises the issues that will be taken up in the remainder of the dialogue, the two most important of which are: What is justice, and why should anyone prefer being just rather being unjust? To answer these questions, Socrates suggests that he and his conversation partners construct a hypothetical "city in speech," an ideal city that they agree is just. (The Greek word for "city" is *polis*, which is the root of the word *political*. The *polis* was the basic political community in ancient Greece. For us, it is the "state.") Because a city is a large structure, this perfectly just city, even if it exists only in thought, will allow the nature of justice itself to become an object of study. The second part of the *Republic,* which is found in Books II–IV, is thus, devoted to the "construction" of an ideal political regime.

The regime Socrates constructs is a tightly controlled one, in which cultural activity is strictly regulated, poetry is censored, physical education is emphasized, a rigid class system is enforced, and the private family is eliminated. Needless to say, these proposals will cause readers to object. Readers will find, however, that even if they disagree with what Socrates recommends, developing arguments against his proposals is a most valuable exercise. They will be forced to think through basic assumptions concerning politics in this course. For example, almost all of us believe that political freedom is a good thing and that all citizens should be counted as equal before the law. But why? Plato will encourage us to defend our most cherished beliefs.

Unlike in a democracy, where rulers are elected on the basis of their popular appeal, in Socrates's regime, the only criterion for ruling is being extremely intelligent and knowledgeable, or as he puts it, being "wise." Because of this, the *Republic* takes a gigantic detour. In order to understand what it means to be a ruler, one must understand what wisdom is. For this reason, the third part of the *Republic*, Books V–VII, turns away from overtly political questions and concentrates instead on the nature of "philosophy" (which literally means "the love of wisdom"). In this part of the dialogue, Socrates offers some of his most profound and concentrated reflections on philosophical issues. We learn, for example, about the relationship between particulars (such as the beautiful painting that is hanging on the wall) and universals (Beauty itself). We learn about the relationship between the words of our language and the things in the world that these words name. Socrates discusses the nature of mathematics and the difference between images (such as a photograph) and "originals" (the object the photograph is of). He also addresses the single most important principle in all of Plato's philosophy, what he calls "the Idea of the Good," the supreme principle of all reality.

In reading Books V–VII of the *Republic*, students will be exposed to the heart of Platonism. As a consequence, in this course, they will receive an introduction not only to political philosophy but to philosophy in general.

The last part of the *Republic*, Books VIII–X, takes us back to a discussion of politics. Socrates examines those political regimes that are inferior to the ideal. These include the timocracy, a rule by those few men who have achieved honor in battle; oligarchy, rule by the wealthy few; democracy, rule by the people; and tyranny, which is the worst of all possible regimes. This section of the dialogue is rich with insightful observations about "the real world." For example, in discussing oligarchy, we will learn a great deal about the role money plays in people's lives. When Socrates addresses "rule by the people," he will offer some of the sharpest, and most controversial, criticisms of democracy ever written. And when he discusses the tyrant, he will teach us much about the corrupting influence of power.

Throughout the course, we will discuss how reading the *Republic* can generate a discussion of the most pressing contemporary issues. We will, for example, discuss Plato's "medical ethics" and see how they might apply in today's world. We will also discuss how penetrating was his analysis of tyranny, for we will compare what Socrates says about the tyrant to Saddam Hussein.

Reading the 10 books of Plato's *Republic* is like taking a journey. We will move from book to book, from idea to idea, and in doing so, we will touch upon some of the most basic questions that human beings can ask about themselves and the political communities in which they live. This is a comprehensive, a truly great book, and in this course, we will try to study it with the care it deserves.

Lecture Thirteen
Book VI—The Divided Line

Scope:

Socrates's description of the Idea of the Good is alluring but hardly clear. To elaborate and clarify, he draws a figure: a line that is divided into four sections. On one side of the line, he places various cognitive activities: intellection, thought, trust, and imagination. On the other side of the line, he places the objects of these cognitive activities: ideas, mathematical objects, sensible objects, and images. This short passage, which occupies only two pages (509d–511e), is the most concise summary of Plato's conception of reality. Initially, it will seem quite difficult to understand, and although it never becomes crystal clear, by discussing it in detail, it will become accessible.

Outline

I. Socrates draws a "divided line" (509d–511e):

The Idea of the Good

A. Forms (*eidê*)	Intellection (*noêsis*)
B. Mathematical Objects	Thought (*dianoia*)
C. Sensible Things	Trust (*pistis*)
D. Images (*eikones*)	Imagination (*eikasia*)

II. The key to understanding the divided line is to begin at the bottom.

   A. Images are dependent upon sensible things. Sensible things are the "originals" of which images are images.

   1. An example is a shadow and the hand that casts the shadow.

   2. Sensible things are "higher" than images. Images depend on sensible things but not vice versa.

> 3. This relationship between image and original is found throughout the divided line.

B. Sensible things are images of mathematical objects.

> 1. The number 3 can count three apples or three oranges.
>
> 2. The items counted vary, but the number remains constant.
>
> 3. The number is responsible for sensible things being countable and, therefore, for being intelligible.
>
> 4. In this sense, numbers are "higher" than sensible objects.
>
> 5. The extraordinary result of this move is that the sensible world, the world that we trust as most real, is in fact, "only" an image.

C. Mathematical objects are images of Forms.

> 1. This is probably the single most difficult concept to grasp in Plato's *Republic.*
>
> 2. In what way would numbers, for example, depend on Forms?

D. Forms are images of the Idea of the Good.

> 1. It is possible, as many commentators have thought, that "the Good" is "the One."
>
> 2. "The One" is responsible for the intelligibility of all numbers.

III. Because this concept is still extremely hard to understand, Socrates gives an example: the three fingers (523c–d).

A. There are three fingers: the pinky, which is shortest; the ring finger; and the middle finger, which is longest.

B. The ring finger is longer than the pinky but shorter than the middle finger.

> 1. This finger is both longer and shorter.
>
> 2. It is impossible to resolve this contradiction on the level of what Socrates calls "trust," that is, sensation alone. Simply looking at the ring finger does not stop it from being both longer and shorter.

C. For this contradiction to be stabilized, one must count and measure.

1. We can measure the length of the three fingers. Let's say that the pinky is one inch long; the ring finger, two inches; and the middle finger, three inches.

2. What had been a contradiction on the level of "trust" or sensation can be resolved on the level of "thought." We know why the ring finger is both longer and shorter: It is two inches long.

D. The simple act of counting and measuring implies the movement up the line from level C to level B.

1. This is the move when the sensible world, which we normally take for granted, is transformed into an image of a higher reality.

2. Perhaps the best way to understand what Socrates has in mind is to think of a law of physics. It is expressed in a mathematical formula, but it makes intelligible the way things move.

E. The extraordinary move from B to A, from mathematical objects to Forms, is an extension of this move.

1. This move requires resistance to "intellectual gravity," from the temptation to move back down from B to C. The "arts," or *technê*, which are those subjects that use applied mathematics, move downward.

2. Philosophy is a turning around, a moving upward when ordinary thought would normally move downward. It is a search for ultimate intelligible structures of reality.

IV. How should we define the notion of *dialectic* (511b)?

A. When the philosopher has worked his or her way up to the top of the line, namely to the Idea of the Good, he or she then goes back down.

B. But this downward journey is not like that of the arts.

C. This is what Socrates calls *dialectic*.

1. "Making no use of anything sensed in any way, but using forms themselves, going through forms to forms, it ends in forms too" (511c).

2. Again, it is very difficult to understand what this means.

3. The divided line seems to offer an image of what the philosophical project is. It is a formal articulation of the whole of reality.

Essential Reading:

Plato's Republic, Book VI.

Supplementary Reading:

Annas, J. *An Introduction to Plato's Republic*, pp. 242–272.

Howland, J. *The Republic: The Odyssey of Philosophy*, pp. 119–149.

Klein, J. *A Commentary on Plato's Meno*, pp. 115–125.

Mitchell, B., and J. R. Lucas. *An Engagement with Plato's Republic*, pp. 88–106.

Roochnik, D. *Beautiful City: The Dialectical Character of Plato's Republic*, pp. 34–40.

Roochnik, D. *Retrieving the Ancients*, pp. 126–134.

Questions to Consider:

1. Do all images depend on some "original"? In other words, are all images "images of something"?

2. Socrates implies that the sensible world is no more than an image of a higher, non-sensible reality. Does this idea of a "higher reality" make sense to you?

Lecture Thirteen—Transcript
Book VI—The Divided Line

In the previous lecture we discussed the famous—or perhaps the infamous—Idea of the Good, this is Plato's supreme principle; it's the supreme principle of reality, of being, of knowledge and of truth. It's a terribly obscure passage as we saw. It's obscure not because the descriptions of it are so extraordinarily complicated; in fact, they're not. What they are is extraordinarily sparse. Socrates, in fact, tells us very little about the Idea of the Good. In the last lecture, I gave you a couple of speculations as to why Plato writes this scene in this way. Perhaps, I suggested, he's trying to provoke the reader into thinking for himself or for herself. Those were speculations and no more. Socrates himself acknowledges that this discussion of the Idea of the Good is obscure or is, at least, insufficient. His colleague, Glaucon, is puzzled and, of course, why shouldn't he be; it's a terribly puzzling description. So Socrates tries to help out. He helps out by means of an image. It's the image that's become known by scholars as the "Divided-Line," which will be the focus of today's lecture.

I need to warn you in advance that once again we will be in some murky waters. This is a very difficult passage to understand, it's again very sparse when you read it on your own, and you'll perhaps be surprised by how quickly it goes by. And you won't really be able to understand each and every move that Socrates makes. I'll do my best to try to explain, at the same time, I'll also have to do some interpreting in this passage; I'll alert you when I'm offering you some of my own views about how to understand the Divided-Line.

Socrates gives Glaucon instructions about how to draw a certain line. In ancient Greece, they had no blackboards, and they had no projectors; so the line probably would have been drawn in the sand right at their feet. So let's try to imagine these instructions being given to us, in fact, you could even follow these instructions yourself at home with just paper and pencil. Take a line and divide it into two unequal sections. Socrates doesn't tell us which of the sections, the top section or the bottom section. Notice I'm assuming that the line is vertical, we learn later that it is vertical, but actually here in this passage, Socrates doesn't even tell us that it's vertical; again, however, we'll assume it is, and we get evidence for this later. We have our vertical line; we cut it into two unequal segments. Then we cut each of the unequal segments again, following the same proportion of the original cut.

What you have before you, if you have undergone this exercise with Socrates, is a line with four sections. We can label the top section A, then B, then C, and the bottom section can be labeled D. One of the things you'll notice right away on your drawing, even if you did it very quickly, is that the two middle sections, regardless of how you cut the line yourself, are equal. We can prove this. In the translation that I use, that by Allan Bloom, in his notes he shows you the proof. Whatever translation you are using, it's likely you'll find this discussion in the notes. The two middle sections are equal, and that turns out in my interpretation of the Divided-Line, to be very important.

The line is vertical; therefore, it has a left side and a right side. Socrates labels each of these four segments and each side of the lines. On the left side, we find objects. The objects are as follows, and you can follow this as I diagram it in the booklet that accompanies the course. If you're using Allan Bloom's translation, as I am, you'll see this is similar to the drawing he uses. Any translation, again, that you're using, will likely have a figure accompanying this passage of the *Republic*. On the left at the top—this would be section A—are forms, in Greek the word is *eidê*. You see that in the booklet, that it's the plural of *eidos*. Section B, the second segment, is mathematical objections. Section C, below that, is sensible things. Section D, the very bottom on the left, is images or *eikones*. I pronounce that word you see the Greek in the booklet to remind you that it's the root of our word, icon or image. On the right side of the line, corresponding to each of these four objects is a psychological or cognitive state that is responsible for apprehending the object. Corresponding to forms, on the left, is intellection on the right. The Greek is pronounced *noêsis*. Corresponding to mathematical objects on the right is thought, *dianoia*. Corresponding to sensible things, is trust, in Greek the word is *pistis*. Corresponding to the images is imagination, or *eikasia*. This is all very mysterious at this point, so let's try to figure it out.

A very great scholar, who's name was Jacob Klein—his work you'll find in the bibliography in the booklet—made a suggestion about how to understand the Divided-Line, which I have long followed and I will be imitating his argument in the way I present the material that

I hope will elucidate the meaning of the Divided-Line. Klein's suggestion is that the key to understanding the Divided-Line is to start at the bottom, with images. So let's think about images for just a couple of minutes.

We need to think about images, D on the left at the bottom, in relationship to C, sensible things, which are above the images. The key point is this: an image is an image of something. Best example, the example Socrates himself uses, is a shadow. A shadow is an image of a sensible thing, which is responsible for producing the shadow. An example that would come very quickly to our minds, of course, would be a photograph. If I take a picture of you with a camera, the picture is the image; you are the original. You are a sensible thing, a real thing, and the image is an image of you. I mention that this line needs to be vertical, and the reason why is because sensible things are higher than images. Now, what does higher mean? It means that images are dependent upon sensible things. If I remove my hand, there is no shadow. It doesn't work the other way around. If I cut off the light source, there's no shadow, but there's still a hand. The sensible original is responsible for the image; the image is dependent on the original. Klein's thesis, which I believe is accurate, is that this relationship between image and original works its way through the entire Divided-Line. Let's move up to see what that means.

Sensible things—my hand, the chair, and the table—are themselves, images of mathematical objects. In terms of the diagram that you have in your booklet, sensible things is segment C; mathematical objects, section B. That is not an obvious description is it, to say that sensible things are images of mathematical objects. In fact, it's a rather difficult move to understand.

Let me offer you this suggestion, this example, as a way of thinking about this. Let's just pick a number, the number 3. The number 3 is capable of counting 3 apples, or 3 oranges, 3 grapefruits, or 3 tables. The number 3 remains the same, the number 3 is not something we can touch with our hands or see with our eyes; it's a concept, it's an intelligible structure. The chairs, the tables, the oranges, the apples, they can all change; I can substitute an apple for an orange, the apple can go bad or become rotten and actually disappear, but the number 3 remains constant. The number 3, you might say, has a kind of power that sensible things don't have, and this is the sense in which sensible things are themselves, images of higher originals, namely mathematical objects. This is still, I would guess, rather difficult to follow.

Numbers, according to Plato, are responsible for sensible things being intelligible. He would argue, and he may well be right, that the world of our senses, the world that comes into our eyes and we feel with our hands, would simply make no sense whatsoever unless we could count. He takes counting very, very seriously. You'll see in the next couple of lectures that mathematics, and arithmetic in particular, will start to gain more and more prominence in Plato's *Republic*.

Once again, mathematical objects, and we'll focus exclusively on an example of numbers, are higher than sensible objects. Sensible objects are images. If this is true, and I would ask you to entertain this possibility for the next few minutes, an extraordinary thing has happened. The sensible world, the world that we normally think of as being real, the world we're most comfortable with, the world which we trust—that's the word that is on the right side of the line corresponding to sensible things—that world that we typically take for granted, has become transformed as we moved from C to B; it has become transformed into an image. Go back to the bottom of the line to understand what this means. This shadow is an image of the hand. The hand is more real than the shadow; I know that because if I remove the hand, the shadow disappears. The shadow depends on the hand for its reality.

Socrates is making the extraordinary suggestion that the sensible world is like a shadow. It's dependent on a higher form of reality. In this case, in this particular segment of the Divided-Line, that form of the reality is mathematical. This is an extraordinary discovery on Plato's part, and you'll perhaps recall a point I made when I asked you to actually draw the Divided-Line; the two segments of the Divided-Line that are in the middle, B and C, are equal. Regardless of how you divide the line, they always have to be equal. I think this is a point that Plato is trying to communicate. It's a point that was made much, much later by someone like the great physicist Galileo. Galileo famously said the book of nature is written in the characters of mathematics. What did he mean by that? He meant, I think, precisely what Socrates means here, that the sensible world, the world that we observe, is itself structured by mathematical principles. The deeper reality of the sensible world is found, not in what we can touch with our hands, but in what we can think with our minds and principally, in what we can think by way of mathematics. Corresponding to mathematical objects on the right side of the line is that word thought. This is how we access reality. Again, this is a rather puzzling idea that we don't get our basic contact with reality with our senses. We get it with our minds, a fundamental tenant of Platonism.

We move up the line. We move from segment B to segment A, from mathematical objects to forms. We've already talked a lot about forms in this course. Here they are at the top of the Divided-Line, although not at the very top. Yet, they're very close to the top. Unfortunately, once again, Socrates is very reticent about the relationship between forms and mathematical objects. Still, we can infer what he means if, once again, we take our bearings from the bottom of the line.

His point, I believe, is this: mathematical objects, which are the originals of which sensible things are images, are themselves, images of forms. Forms are the higher level of reality, the more basic originals of which mathematical objects are merely images. The Divided-Line, in short, is a very compact picture of all of reality. At the top of the ontological hierarchy—ontological is the word that is derived from the Greek word for being—are the forms. I'm not going to try to explain any further the relationship between forms and mathematical objects; this is a theme we will come back to shortly, however.

At the very top of the Divided-Line, what do we find? Socrates doesn't quite say it explicitly, be he clearly intends it. This is, of course, the Idea of the Good. So now, pushing our idea of image and original to the top of the Divided-Line, we can say what? That even forms, the form of beauty, the form of justice, the subject of the *Republic* itself, even these forms are images of the highest principle of all the Idea of the Good. As we know, and we discussed in the previous lecture, we're just not sure of what Plato means by the Idea of the Good.

Many commentators throughout the history of philosophy have made a suggestion that's plausible, but certainly not provable, and that is that the Idea of the Good is what came to be known as "the One." The Idea of the Good is the One, the principle of unity. This is an attractive proposal if you think in the following terms. The idea of the one is itself responsible for the possibility of any number. If I have the number 3, I can conceive of the number 3 as 3 ones. In Greek arithmetic, ancient Greek arithmetic, 1 was not a number; the first number was 2. That's because in the Greek mind, a number was a number of ones. If I count three apples, an apple is functioning as my unit, and I count 1, 2, 3 apples. The unit must come first and I think this might be the reasoning behind those commentators that believe that the Idea of the Good is really the One. That before we can even begin to think, either mathematically or in terms of forms, we must begin with the idea. We must think of the most basic idea of all, which is the idea of the unit, of oneness. If this is true, then we will identify the one as the ultimate principle responsible for the intelligibility of all of the rest of reality.

This is still, needless to say, rather hard to understand. Socrates appreciates that. One of the great benefits of writing a dialogue, as Plato does, is by giving Socrates a conversation partner, in this case Glaucon. He often will have Glaucon ask questions, the very same questions we readers ourselves would likely ask, and Glaucon doesn't understand everything that Socrates has been saying. Later, and I refer here to 523c–d, which is in Book VII—the Divided-Line you recall occurs at the very end of Book VI—Socrates tries to explain the Divided-Line a little more elaborately and he gives an example.

He asks us to imagine three fingers. The pinky finger is the little finger, the ring finger is in between, and then the middle finger is the largest finger. You don't have to think about this in terms of fingers, just imagine—again, you might even want to sketch with pencil and paper—three lines, where you go from the shortest to the middle to the longest line. The key point Socrates makes here is that the finger in the middle—when I say middle, I'm not referring to the middle finger, I'm referring to the in-between finger, the finger that's larger than the smallest, and smaller than the largest—that finger, if I simply look at it with my eyes, is both larger and smaller. It's both longer and shorter. Socrates identifies this as a contradiction. This doesn't make sense, how can something be both longer and shorter? His point that he makes in Book VII is that with my eyes alone, with my senses, I cannot resolve this contradiction. You can prove this by just looking at those three little lines with a pencil and paper, and just focus. First I look at the middle line in relationship to the smaller, and then in relationship to the bigger, and you'll of course see, exactly what Socrates means, that middle line is both longer and shorter, and that's a contradiction. A contradiction, according to Socrates, doesn't make sense.

Another way to put this point then, is that the information we get with our eyes, by itself just doesn't make sense. So what do we do? We need to stabilize; we need to make intelligible what is otherwise unintelligible on the level of sensation. How do we do it? We do it very easily, very common-sensically. We measure the three fingers or the three lines that we've drawn. We'll say that the smallest is two inches long, the middle is three inches long, and the longest is four inches long; 2, 3, and 4 inches. Now, having made that measurement, my otherwise contradictory sensations have been resolved. They've been rendered intelligible. They've been stabilized.

What had been unintelligible is now intelligible. This is a way of going back to the Divided-Line, and recall what corresponds to sensible things on the right is trust. What we normally trust to be reliable is the information we get from our senses. Socrates's point is that that's just not the way it is. What's much more reliable is the way we think about the information we receive from our senses. That primary act of thinking is found in counting, in measuring. By establishing the exact length of the three fingers or the three lines, I am moving upwards from C to B; I'm realizing that numbers are actually more powerful in explaining reality than what I receive through my eyes. This very simple act, utterly common-sensical act, is, in fact, of fundamental philosophical importance for Plato; it suggests the point I made earlier, that the sensible world itself is but an image of a higher reality.

Now, let met go back to the observation I made about the geometry of line, namely, that those two middle sections are equal. Once we have moved up from sensible things to mathematical objects, the two segments that are exactly equal in length, there's a very great temptation; it's a temptation we all know. It's the temptation to go back down. The reason why we're so tempted to go back down is because, as we all know, mathematics is so remarkably useful in explaining, even manipulating the sensible world. If I'm a carpenter and I know a little bit about geometry, I'm able to use that knowledge to help me build a house. If I'm a merchant and I know arithmetic, I can use that knowledge to help me make money. On a vastly more sophisticated level, I will return to my comparison with Galileo. In mathematical physics, I learn my mathematics, I learn the laws of nature that are mathematical, and I can return to the sensible world and know how it works and be able to manipulate it.

This going back down from B to C, I like to think of as intellectual gravity. The weight of thinking seems to pull us downwards, precisely because mathematics is so useful in manipulating the sensible world. Socrates gives a word to describe this tendency of thought; he calls it the *technê*, the arts, the crafts. That word is the root of our word technology, or technical. His point, then, is that technical thinking is the application of mathematics to the sensible world in order to achieve useful, practical results.

Again, I would use the phrase intellectual gravity to describe this tendency to move from B to C. The point Socrates wants to make, however, is that the goal of the philosopher is to reverse intellectual gravity and to go upwards rather than downwards, instead of moving from mathematical objects back down to sensible things, to move upwards from mathematical objects to the forms, to turn around. I use that phrase with some emphasis because this will become very important in our next lecture when we discuss, in some detail, the platonic conception of education. The goal of the philosopher is to resist the temptation, to resist the temptation to use the results of thinking to achieve practical results in the sensible word. The name Socrates gives for this upward thrust of intellectual labor is dialectic. You'll see that at 511b. The challenge is to go upwards from mathematical objects to the forms, to the very top of the line. The Idea of the Good, then, and I'm going to quote 511c, is "to work our way, all the way back down the entire line, making no use of anything sensed in any way, but using forms themselves, going through forms, to forms, it ends in forms too."

Again, it's very difficult to understand exactly what Socrates means. I've read this passage hundreds of times and I'm not sure, I will confess that. However, I think at least we can get a sense of what he means. Dialectic is the process of completely reversing intellectual gravity, understanding that even mathematics is merely images of higher intelligible realities, the forms in which themselves are images of the good or perhaps the one. Upon understanding that, we can work our way down through all the remaining categories, or segments of reality, and give an explanation of everything, in terms of those higher principles.

In short, the Divided-Line seems to offer an image of philosophy itself. It suggests the possibility of a formal articulation of the whole of reality. For one clue as to what this might mean in more concrete terms, let's go back to the very beginning of the *Republic* when Socrates asks Cephalus what seems to be such a simple question. He asks him, what is justice? We've discussed this idea several times in the course already. That question is a way of looking for the form of justice. This is a question that is seeking a universal definition, an intelligible structure. It's a question that disparages the particulars. The particulars are those individual, sensible things that come into being and then pass away, trees and dogs and cats, apples and oranges. Those, in a very important sense, are of little interest to Socrates. What he's interested in is the formal structure, the intelligible structure, of reality and not the particulars that seem to populate reality. That he relegates the level merely of sense.

Lecture Fourteen
Book VII—The Parable of the Cave

Scope:

Perhaps because he realizes how difficult it was for Glaucon and Adeimantus—and for us, the readers—to understand the Idea of the Good and the divided line, Socrates tells another parable: that of the cave. It is an extended image that is meant to explain the extraordinarily abstract material we have discussed in the previous four lectures and to reconnect the philosophical concerns of this section with the general concern with politics that animated the dialogue from the beginning.

We are like prisoners in cave, shackled and forced to stare at a wall on which are projected shadows cast by objects illuminated by a fire. The process of education is a turning around, a seeing of reality for what it is. When a prisoner is liberated, he or she—and don't forget that Socrates is a feminist!—goes upward and sees the fire that has been responsible for the shadows. Finally, the prisoner makes it to the world above, where he or she sees the sun—and don't forget that the sun is an image of the Idea of the Good! We will explore the parable in detail.

Outline

I.   The parable of the cave can be outlined as follows (514a-521b):

   A. There are prisoners in a cave, whose legs and necks are chained so that they can only face forward.

   B. On the wall in front of them are images, which are shadows cast by puppets being carried behind the prisoners. A fire provides the light that causes the shadows to appear on the wall.

   C. These "strange prisoners" are "like us" (515a).

      1. This is a reference to the divided line.

      2. Most human beings treat sensible objects as if they were real, when in fact, they are images.

3. This is what Socrates meant by "trust." We trust—that is, we unreflectively believe—that what we can see, hear, touch, taste, and smell is real.

D. The cave is something like a contemporary movie theatre.

1. This comparison between the cave and a movie theatre is meant to provoke reflection on the monumental role images play in contemporary culture.

2. We live in a world of TV, computers, movies—visual images.

II. Education is a "turning around."

A. A prisoner is released and "compelled" (515c) to stand up and turn around.

1. This is a painful procedure.

2. The prisoner is "dazzled" when he looks at the fire: He cannot see clearly.

3. Eventually, the prisoner must admit that what he had thought was real is not.

B. The prisoner is "dragged" (515e) out of the cave and forced into the light of the sun.

C. Gradually, he becomes able to see the things of the "real world" without pain.

1. Eventually, he can even glance at the sun.

2. The sun represents the Idea of the Good.

D. Philosophical education is not the accumulation of new information. It is, instead, a "revolution," a turning around.

1. Philosophical education requires the student to become fundamentally suspicious of conventional conceptions of reality.

2. Perhaps this is why Socrates uses so many images and tells stories: to inspire the student to turn around.

III. The liberated prisoner is unwilling to return to the cave.

A. The liberated prisoner is "compelled" (519c) to return to the cave in order to illuminate it. The parable of the cave is the story of "enlightenment."

B. Glaucon wonders whether forcing the liberated prisoner, who is the philosopher, to return to the cave is unjust. (See 519d.)

C. Socrates responds that the goal is not the happiness or well-being of any individual citizen but the well-being of the whole city. Therefore, the liberated prisoners—that is, the philosophers—will be forced to return to the cave and rule.

    1. A basic principle to be derived here is that the best city is the one ruled by those who are least eager to rule.

    2. A basic requirement for a well-governed city is that within it, there must be a conception of a life better than the political life and a conception of reality that is better than human or political reality (521a).

IV. An interesting exercise is to map all the objects in the cave parable on to the divided line. The following questions may make this more difficult to do:

A. Who are the "puppet-handlers" (514a)?

B. What does the fire represent?

C. What is the value of seeing the sun to prisoners in a cave?

D. Must an injustice be done to the philosopher? If so, is there a serious flaw in the *Republic*?

Essential Reading:

Plato's Republic, Book VII.

Supplementary Reading:

Howland, J. *The Republic: The Odyssey of Philosophy*, pp. 132–149.

Questions to Consider:

1. Do you spend a lot of time watching TV and on the Internet? If so, are you aware of the role images play in your life?

2. Do we really want a leader who is "above" the citizens?

Lecture Fourteen—Transcript
Book VII—The Parable of the Cave

The last two lectures have been remarkably abstract. It's easy, perhaps, to forget that this dialogue is titled the *Republic*. The Greek word is *politeia*, related to our word politics. It's a very reasonable question to ask at this stage of our study, what in the world does all this abstract philosophizing have to do with politics? What does it have to do with justice?

Socrates, at the beginning of Book VII, begins the process of answering that question, of returning us to the basic issues of politics. He does so here, at the beginning of Book VII, by reciting what has become one of the most famous little stories or parables in the history of western philosophy. It's the parable of the cave and it runs from 514a–521b. This is a story that many high-school students study, and it's well known to many people throughout all levels of education. I use the word education there deliberately, because the cave, says Socrates, is meant to be an image of education. We know from the very beginning of the *Republic* that education has been a major concern of Socrates. The cave is an image of it; it's a way of summarizing his basic thoughts about education.

Construct the following image in your minds: use your imagination and imagine prisoners in a cave. Their legs and their necks are shackled and, as a result, they are unable to turn their heads. They're forced to look in one direction only, at the wall in front of them. On the wall in front of them are projected images. These images are generated by puppets that are behind them. They can't see these puppets, because their necks are shackled. There is a fire behind these puppets that is casting the shadows on the wall. This is a very strange image. As always, whatever you end up thinking about Plato as a philosopher, you won't be able to deny the fact that he's a marvelous writer, and in this case, he's a marvelous storyteller. These are very strange people down at the bottom of a cave. Nonetheless, says Socrates, they are like us. He uses those exact words at 515a.

In what conceivable way could they be like us? Well, I think we're prepared to answer that question, because we've just studied the Divided-Line, and we paid particular attention to the issue of images. These prisoners, who are like us, are seeing images. They, because they can't turn their heads, don't know that they're seeing images; they think they're seeing reality, when, in fact, all that is in front of them is shadows. They are like us because we treat the sensible world in the same way. We, ordinary people, tend to believe that what we can touch with our hands and see with our eyes is reality. You recall from the Divided-Line that corresponding to sensible objects on the left side of the line is trust on the right side. I think now we're in a position to understand that word. We trust reality. We trust the reports that we get from our senses and believe that what we're seeing actually exists. In doing so, we're like prisoners who are trapped in the world of images. We just don't know that they are images.

One way of thinking about the cave is to imagine a movie theater. It's very similar, actually; if you think of a darkened movie theater, everybody is looking at the screen and the projector is behind them. As the movie gets more and more enthralling, you absolutely forget that there is a projector behind you, and you are treating these images—this spectacle in front of your eyes—as if it were reality. This is why we can cry or cheer at a movie; we forget it's only an image. I make this comparison between the parable of the cave and the modern-day movie theater, because certainly in our day and age, we live in a world that's increasingly dominated by images. If Plato were to appear on our streets in today's world, I think he'd be just astonished at the ubiquitous presence of images. Of course we spend so much time on our computers, on the Internet, on TV, and with DVDs, that we are very easily trapped into thinking that these images that we see with our eyes are, in fact, reality. Plato would caution us and say, be careful, don't become intoxicated with your images; don't become so dependent on your screens. As a university professor I'm always struck by the need that modern-day students have for visual images to accompany lectures. They're very impatient with lectures that don't have all sorts of spectacles going on with it.

Education, for Socrates, is turning around. This is the dominant metaphor of the parable of the cave. You will perhaps even remember at the very beginning of Plato's *Republic*, Socrates is headed home to Athens proper and he is forced to turn around and come back into the Piraeus with Polemarchus. As is often the case in Book I that was a foreshadowing of the story of the cave.

The main idea that Socrates tries to communicate in his imagery of education is that it requires a certain kind of force. A prisoner—and we're all prisoners, prisoners of images—a prisoner must be "compelled," a word you find at 515c, to stand up and turn around and start to make his or her way out of the cave. Obviously, there has to be a compulsion of some sort, because for one thing, these prisoners have been locked into their positions. They need assistance in unloosening their bonds, and it's going to be very painful. Just treat this image at face value for a second and you'll know, of course, that if you've been sitting a long time and if your head hasn't been turning, if you've been, for example, on an airplane for a long flight, it's very painful to get up and move around; it's painful at first.

That is, says Socrates, exactly what education is like; it's painful. It's painful for another reason. When this prisoner is liberated by some sort of teacher and forced to turn around and start to make way upwards out of the cave, the prisoner will see the puppets, and the prisoner will see the fire that is casting the shadows. This is going to be painful in more than one sense. It's going to be painful because the light from the fire will be rather difficult to look at. You know what happens when you move from a darkened space into a more illuminated space; it hurts your eyes. It will be painful in another deeper sense, however. It will be painful because the prisoner, who is not liberated, will realize that what he had taken to be reality, these images flickering before his eyes, wasn't reality at all. This is a terrible experience that students have to go through. They have to realize that what they thought was true, is in fact, not true. What they thought was real, perhaps isn't so real. What they thought was reality, in fact, was only an image. Exactly the language we were developing in our study of the Divided-Line.

In fact, says Socrates, 515e, the prisoner has to be dragged out of the cave. Once reaching the top, getting into the surface of the earth, the prisoner will be bathed in sunlight, and this, again, will be terribly painful. The sun, of course, is even much brighter than the fire. It will take a while for the prisoner's eyes to become adjusted to the bright light. Eventually, those eyes will become accustomed to it, and at that point, the prisoner is no longer a prisoner, the prisoner sees reality for what it is. The prisoner will see trees and animals and the moon and the stars and, in fact, eventually will even be able to glimpse the sun itself. You remember our discussion of the Idea of the Good. The sun is, Socrates says, the child of the good. The sun is analogous to the good. This is clearly at work in the cave story. The process of education starts at the bottom of the cave, where we are only surrounded by images. It ends up traversing the various stages of the Divided-Line, until we reach the top, the sun, or analogously, the Idea of the Good.

I think it's important here to take a step back and reflect on this metaphor that Socrates develops in order to express his conception of education. Education is turning around. Let me suggest to you a competing image of education, which I think will shed some light on Socrates' conception of education. This is, I would say unfortunately, the image of education we live with in our time. I think, for us, education tends to be conceived as the reception of information. We live, we're told, many, many times, in the information age. You can go onto your Internet connection and get all the information you want; the computer is astonishing at providing it for us. I sometimes think of this conception of education as the empty-head conception of education. Think of your head being opened up and information, data, facts, are just poured into the empty head. Very often students who are quite accustomed to this model of education will sit rather passively in a university course and just take notes. They are accustomed to the professor dispensing facts, dispensing little tiny bits of wisdom, which they receive.

The Socratic model is very different. This is a conception of education as turning around. This is a conception of education as revolutionary, because that, in fact, is what revolution means, a turning around. It's a conception of education that requires great struggle, and in fact, requires pain. You remember that this prisoner has to be dragged out of the cave. What that suggests is that the Socratic goal of education, and I believe we already know this about Socrates from our studies so far, is to make us uncomfortable. It's to make us uncomfortable with conventional reality, uncomfortable with traditional opinions. The overwhelming, philosophical demand is to think for oneself. This is not easy, because when you think for yourself, you challenge conventional wisdom; you try to move upwards on the Divided-Line, you are unwilling to treat images as reality, and demand that reality be treated as reality.

I think this is a very useful way of shedding some light on Socrates as a character in Plato's dialogue. Socrates, as we now know, is a rather strange person. I would take you all the way back to the opening scene of the *Republic* for a reminder. The first thing he does when he meets the old man, Cephalus, is to ask him what's it like to be so old. How does it feel to be close to death? This is a question that conventional manners would certainly prohibit most of us from asking. Socrates is aggressive. At times, he's almost crude in the bluntness of his questioning. I think we now can get a sense of why he acts this way. He is trying to destabilize us. He's trying to shake us up, get us to think for ourselves, get us to make a break with what everybody else has been telling us. If Socrates were to appear on our streets today, I think he would say, especially to young people, unplug those computers of yours. They're wonderful at dispensing little bits of information, very impressive tools indeed, however, that's not the same thing as thinking. Real thinking goes on inside of your minds, it requires effort; it requires even this painful procedure that's described in the cave.

After the prisoner is fully liberated and is bathing in the sunshine of the real world on top, something strange again happens. The liberated prisoner is compelled, 519c, to return to the cave in order to share his illumination. The cave is perhaps the single best story in the history of western philosophy that expresses the theme of enlightenment. I mean, with that word, something very literal, bringing light. The prisoner is forced to return to the cave in order to shed light in that darkness. This is, of course, the philosopher king or the philosopher queen. We have been talking about such a person for sometime now. This is the person, the philosopher who understands the Idea of the Good, which is mimicked by the sun in the parable of the cave, and who brings that understanding into the cave or, to put it another way, into the city—the *polis*—in order to help bring the polis up; to bring justice, to bring goodness, and to make it a better place.

Glaucon, who is never reluctant to ask a hard question, objects. He says, wait a minute Socrates, isn't this rather unfair to the philosopher? We're forcing the philosopher, who is bathing in the sunshine, to go back into this dark, smoky cave. Aren't we, Glaucon asks—and I'm referring to line 519d—aren't we doing the philosopher an injustice? We're making him or her do something that's contrary to their nature. Perhaps you remember that the basic principle of Socrates' city—and this goes all the way back to the first city that we discussed in Book II—is the idea of the division of labor. You recall the simplest city has only four or five people, the shoemaker, the farmer, the carpenter, etc. The shoemaker must be good at making shoes. We would never ask a shoemaker to become a carpenter, and we wouldn't ask a carpenter to become a farmer.

Implicit in Glaucon's question, then, is the objection that the philosopher is being treated unfairly or unjustly because he or she is now being required to do two jobs. First job is to be a philosopher. It's a very hard job; you have seen some of the difficulties involved with it by reading the Divided-Line and the Idea of the Good passages. The second job that the philosopher is now being forced to do, is to rule the city. So which is it, what is the philosopher's job? Is it to be a philosopher or to rule the city? It's not just, Glaucon says, to ask philosophers to do both. Some commentators say that this is actually a fatal flaw in Plato's entire project and we'll come back to that issue.

Perhaps you can image Socrates' response to Glaucon's objection. It's very similar to his reasoning that we've encountered many times in the *Republic*. He says to Glaucon, the happiness of any one individual, whether it's the philosopher or anyone else, is not my concern, I'm trying to construct a just city, a perfectly good city, and my overriding concern is the goodness of the whole, not the goodness of any individual. So if the philosopher would rather bathe in the sunshine, too bad. The demands of the city require that the philosopher rule the city. This is the famous third wave we discussed earlier. So therefore, justice, says Socrates objecting to Glaucon's objection, justice requires the philosopher to be forced to go back into the cave, into the city.

In this context, Socrates makes two comments that I think are very interesting and worth thinking about. These comments come right out of the parable of the cave story. He says, at 520d, and I'll paraphrase it, the best city, and in fact, the only really good city, can be one in which those who rule are least eager to rule. I think we should think about this statement a little bit further. Recall a comment I made earlier about democracy, which is always on Plato's mind in the *Republic*. In a democracy, whether it's an American democracy or an Athenian democracy, opposing candidates always have one thing in common: they want the job. They want to be elected. In American politics, it's so hard to get elected. The campaigns are so long, they require such monumental effort, that only someone, whether Democrat or Republican, who is hugely in love with the idea of being president, can manage to go through with such an arduous campaign. So this is a situation that's the opposite of that, what Socrates thinks is required for a truly just city. If there is going to be a successful city, the person who rules must be like the liberated prisoner, who would much prefer to stay up on earth, bathing in the sun, than to come down and actually rule.

In the same vein, Socrates says the following at 521a, and I'll quote this directly: "If you discover a life better than ruling, for those who are going to rule, it is possible that your well governed city will come into being." This is very much the same point. In order for a truly good city to exist, there must be a kind of life that's better than ruling. Let me try to give you some suggestions about this line. To do so, I'll go back to an earlier theme that we discussed when were discussing the Idea of the Good.

You recall a comment Socrates makes about the Idea of the Good. If we don't know what it is, nothing else that we have is really good. I used the example of money as a way of illustrating this principle. Socrates's point is that money is not good or bad; money, despite the fact that it seems very good to most people, is actually neutral. If you have a lot of money, you can use it well and be benefited, or if you have a lot of money, you can use it very badly and it will damage you. So it's neither good nor bad; it's neither beneficial nor harmful; it's neutral. In order to make it good, we must know how to use it, and in order to know how to use it, we must have some access to the Idea of the Good. Now, I'm discussing money because I think the point is exactly parallel to the one Socrates makes about ruling.

If there were nothing else in the world except money as a good, then the quest for money would be endless. If I had a million dollars, it wouldn't be enough; I'd want two million dollars. If I had a hundred million dollars, I'd want two hundred million dollars, and on and on it would go. Money would simply beget money. I think Socrates' point is very similar about political power, political rule. If there were no guiding principle, no higher life, no greater good than political power, then political power would have no objective other than itself. What would happen if there was no higher objective? Then, political power would want to do nothing else except expand. This is a kind of diagnosis of expansionism. There are regimes—and Socrates would think of Sparta, perhaps he'd even think of Athens itself in the 5th century—whose only objective is to get bigger, to expand itself, to see itself and bring itself into other countries. This is a catastrophe, according to Socrates. This can never be just, because just like the quest for money never ends, and therefore, can never be satisfied; so too would the quest for political power, if there were no higher principle to guide it, never be satisfied, never be just.

Or think of the argument that Socrates makes against hedonism. Remember the definition of hedonism: it's the position that pleasure is the highest good. Socrates says, when he's discussing the Idea of the Good, that the majority of people, the *hoi polloi*, they very frequently believe that the pleasure is the good. For Socrates, that's a catastrophic mistake, because Socrates believes that there's a distinction to be made between good pleasures and bad pleasures. If there's a distinction between good and bad pleasures, there must be some standard other than pleasure, which measures the goodness of pleasure. If there were no such standard, then the only option available would be to maximize one's pleasures. And that's an endless, unsatisfying, and finally degrading form of life.

Again, the parallel can be made between pleasure and political power. If there were no life better than ruling, then all that would be available would be ruling. If that were the case, the only option for the ruler would be expansion, expansion, and expansion. If I'm ruling a million people today, I want to rule two million people tomorrow. This is a description of the tyrant, who will be discussed at great length shortly in the *Republic*. It is, believes Socrates, a catastrophic fate for a city. Therefore, to go back to these wonderful rich lines at 520d and 521a, it's crucial for the well-being of a political system that there be some goal, some standard, some principle that is itself beyond politics. This is captured beautifully in the parable of the cave. Precisely because the philosopher who reaches the top and gets to enjoy the sun doesn't want to go back into the cave and rule the prisoners, he is most adept and most qualified to do so. The person that is least eager to rule makes the best ruler.

Let me close this lecture by simply listing a few questions or even problems with the parable of the cave. I would give you as an exercise to see if you complete this, try to map all the little objects in the cave story—the shadows, the prisoners, the puppets, the fire—onto the Divided-Line. That's not so easy to do, but it's fun to try. I'll ask some questions though that will make it a bit harder. Who are these puppet handlers, that's a phrase that Socrates uses at 514a.

Well, seemingly these are the people who are responsible for the images. In today's world they might be movie directors or TV producers or web designers. Interesting question, who are they that handle the puppets? What does the fire represent? Fire is an artificial tool in the cave. These are two very difficult questions that are related. Finally, what really is the value of seeing the sun when you come back to the cave? Let's just take the image very seriously. If I see the sun, how will that help me understand what's going on in the cave? Those are two separate worlds. Why does knowing one, help me understand the other? The last question is the one I've already mentioned: must an injustice be done to the philosopher when he or she is forced to return to the cave?

Lecture Fifteen
Book VII—The Education of the Guardians

Scope:

In Book VII, Socrates outlines the curriculum that the guardians study. It is composed of five mathematical subjects—arithmetic, plane geometry, solid geometry, astronomy, and harmonics—and culminates in the study of what Socrates calls *dialectic*. In this lecture, we will concentrate on a general question: Why is mathematics so important in the education of the guardians? Doing so will allow us to review, one last time, the crucial passages concerning the Idea of the Good and the divided line. We will, in other words, complete our overview of Plato's theory of Ideas and his conception of education.

Outline

I.   The *Republic* reaches its pinnacle at the Book VI discussion of the Idea of the Good and the divided line. The descent begins at the beginning of Book VII.

   A. We turn to the specific elements of the education of the philosopher-rulers.

   B. The guardians must study a subject that "draws the soul from becoming to being" (521d).

      1. They begin with "the lowly business of distinguishing the one, the two, and the three. I mean by this, number" (522c).

      2. *Arithmos* is translated as "number." It's the root of *arithmetic*.

      3. The rulers do not study mathematics in order to apply it. Instead, they "turn around."

      4. They engage in the pure, theoretical study of numbers and have no interest in practical or useful benefits of mathematics.

   C. After arithmetic, the rulers study plane geometry, solid geometry, theoretical astronomy, and harmonics.

II. Mathematics plays an important role in Plato's philosophy.

   A. Mathematics is preparation for dialectic.

   B. The theory of Forms projects the qualities of mathematical objects onto "intelligible entities," such as Beauty, Justice, and the Good.

      1. Mathematics is universal and "fair."

      2. Mathematics projects an intelligible realm of agreement and harmony.

      3. The moral-political benefit of mathematics is that it establishes a common project, a shared realm.

      4. Mathematics is a great equalizer. For Plato, this seems to have been an inspiration for learning in general.

      5. For Plato, mathematics is fundamental to a philosophical soul.

      6. Mathematics was important in Plato's Academy.

III. *Dialectic* is the study of Forms and is inspired by the question that Socrates is famous for asking. But dialectic is potentially dangerous (537b–541b).

   A. Dialectic is potentially dangerous for young people: It would encourage them to question conventional wisdom.

      1. An excellent example of this danger is found in Plato's dialogue *The Charmides*.

      2. This dialogue features a promising young man named Charmides, who is accompanied by his uncle, Critias.

      3. Socrates asks, "What is moderation?" This is one of the four cardinal virtues.

      4. Socrates refutes every answer Charmides and Critias offer.

      5. Charmides and Critias later become members of the Tyranny of the Thirty.

   B. Therefore, in Socrates's city, dialectic is reserved for mature people.

IV. Is the just city possible?

   A. Socrates admits that the things he has been discussing about his ideal just city are difficult but not impossible (540b).

B. In the final condition of the possibility of the just city, Socrates advocates that everyone older than 10 must be "sent out to the country" (541a), meaning that they will be killed. The rulers will take over the children.

1. This last condition is horrifying.

2. Does Plato take it seriously? Or is it part of his demonstration that the just city is, in fact, neither possible nor desirable?

Essential Reading:

Plato's Republic, Book VII.

Supplementary Reading:

Mueller, I. "Mathematical Method and Philosophical Truth," in R. Kraut, ed., *The Cambridge Companion to Plato*, pp. 170–199.

Plato, *Charmides*.

Roochnik, D. *Beautiful City: The Dialectical Character of Plato's Republic*, pp. 69–77.

Questions to Consider:

1. Do you think a rigorous training in mathematics is actually the best preparation for a political ruler?

2. Do you think it is dangerous for younger people to engage in dialectic? In other words, is it dangerous for them to ask philosophical questions, or should this activity be encouraged?

Lecture Fifteen—Transcript
Book VII—The Education of the Guardians

Much like the parable of the cave, the *Republic* itself has an ascent and descent structure. We have been consistently ascending. The pinnacle of our ascent was when we reached the sun or, in other words, when we discussed the Idea of the Good and the Divided-Line at the end of Book VI. Now we begin the descent.

We discuss in Book VII, the education of the guardians, the rulers and protectors of the perfectly just city. Now we've known for a long time that education is paramount in Plato's *Republic*, and we've known that the guardians are going to receive a very carefully crafted form of education.

In today's lecture, we'll begin with looking at what you might call the nuts and bolts of this form of education, the actual curriculum that the guardians have to undergo. This is the sense in which I mean we are beginning a descent. No longer are we going to operate at the highest peaks of abstraction and universality, we're beginning our move downwards, back to what most people, rather erroneously call, the real world.

The principle subject that the guardians must study is that subject which affects their soul. Socrates is even more specific. He says, and I'll quote from line 521d, "the guardians must study a subject that draws the soul from becoming to being." Becoming and being are two words we've used before. If you recall, becoming is a region of reality, it's a category of reality. It expresses those kinds of things which come into being and pass out of being, finite, mortal, temporary, transient, fleeting things, the things of the world of our senses. Anything we can touch with our hands or see with our eyes is changing, and anything we can sense will eventually disappear. The other great region of reality is being. The permanent, the changeless, the purely intelligible, that which has no interaction with matter, that which must be thought, but cannot be seen. To reiterate, the guardians need a subject that will, to use what is now a familiar metaphor, turn them around, from becoming to being. This is part of the process of leaving the cave. This is part of the process of ascending up the Divided-Line.

What is this subject? Perhaps, you can predict that it's arithmetic. Socrates, at 522c, identifies this subject by describing it as the lowly business of distinguishing the one, the two, and the three. I mean by this, the number. The Greek word for number is *arithmos*, and it's the root of our word arithmetic, recall a major theme that we discussed in our study of the Divided-Line. The guardians that are undergoing this rigorous form of education do not study mathematics for practical purposes. Of course, this is the way mathematics is studied in most universities today. It was the way most people even would have studied mathematics in ancient Greece; we learn a little bit of math, and then we use it. Not the guardians. The guardians study mathematics, to repeat the metaphor, in order to turn around. They study, and I'm now referring to 525c, the nature of numbers themselves. They're interested not in commerce, they're not interested in technical applications of mathematics, they're interested in the pure study of numbers. In modern language, this is described as number theory.

After they study arithmetic, the guardians study plain geometry, solid geometry, theoretical astronomy, and harmonics. This occupies much of Book VII. In order to understand Book VII and its treatment of these very specific mathematical disciplines, one much study ancient mathematics. It's a very difficult and arcane subject, and I'm not going to discuss it in this lecture. So there will be large passages, which I would much rather treat in a very general manner, and not go into detail.

The main theme of today's lecture is not the specifics of ancient harmonics, although for many people that's an interesting subject, but in a very general sense, the nature of mathematics and why it was so important to Plato. We've already taken good steps towards understanding this in our discussion of the Divided-Line; we're really elaborating on some of the points we discussed then. In a nutshell, again, as we learn from the Divided-Line, mathematics is the best preparation for dialectic, the study of the purely formal structure of the whole of reality.

Let me suggest to you a way of thinking about Plato's understanding of mathematics that might help us understand. In particular, if you go back to the Divided-Line, you'll recall that at level B we find mathematical objects and above that in level A, we find the forms. At the time of discussing it, I suggested that it's really not so obvious what the relationship is between mathematics and the forms. That's what I want to talk about right now for a few minutes.

Let me put the point in the following way: think of the kinds of issues in which we have very real disagreement. You and I might disagree about the painting in the museum, and I say it's beautiful and you say it's ugly. You and I might disagree about a specific tax policy, you might say it's unfair to tax rich people more than we tax poor people, and I might say no, it's perfectly just to do that; we disagree. You might say it's good to give money to charity, I might say it's bad to give money to charity. These are the issues, of course, that human beings have always intensely engaged in conflict over. Now, contrast that realm of disagreement with the realm of mathematics. None of us would ever disagree that two plus two equals four. We take that to be a simple universal objective truth. We take it to be 100% clear that two plus two equals four. Take us back to the museum and imagine the discussion in which we're disagreeing about the beauty of the painting. Well, that's a hard discussion to have because it's not clear what you mean by beauty or what I mean by beauty. Our disagreement about the tax policy, it's not clear what you think justice is or what I think justice is, and that's perhaps the reason why our disagreement goes on for such a long time, and in fact, it seems as if we can't resolve it.

I would suggest that the very best way to think of the relationship between mathematics and the forms—and in turn to understand Plato's deep appreciation of mathematics and the prominent place he gives it in the education of the guardians, because after all, their education seems to be almost exclusively mathematical—is to think of the platonic forms as containing many of the same qualities that mathematics has, but operating in a different sphere. Another word that might be useful here, think of the forms as a projection of mathematical qualities onto issues like beauty and justice. Socrates believes that there is a form of beauty, a form of justice, beauty itself, justice itself. What are they?

They would be the answer to the famous Socratic question, what is beauty, what is justice; they would be forms. They would have precisely the same sorts of qualities that mathematical truth, as we would all agree, already has. These forms would be clear and distinct and universal and objective. This, as we've suggested before, is very hard to imagine. It's very hard to imagine being in a museum and having an intense disagreement about a painting and thinking it could be resolved in the same way that an arithmetic problem can be resolved. If I ask you to multiply 75 times 152, I don't know what the answer to that question is, but I know we will all reach it if we do the steps properly or if we use a calculator, and we will end up with the same answer, and we don't disagree. You and I will not come to blows over that mathematical problem. We may very well, however, come to blows about tax policy. We may disagree so vehemently that we can't find a common ground.

The great platonic hope, the great platonic projection, is to project these kinds of mathematical attributes onto precisely those questions that right now seem to be so far from being resolvable. As I have several times in this course, I'll remind you yet again that in Plato's youth, in the 5th century, he witnessed tremendous turmoil. He witnessed his fellow citizens literally killing each other. This made, without a doubt, an enormous impression on him. Much of his thinking, I think, can be derived from this impulse. How do we resolve conflict? How do we come to harmony among ourselves? The platonic forms may be conceived, in fact, as a hopeful vision in which conflict about those most basic values, the values that people are willing to do die for, values like goodness and justice, can be resolved.

Let me shift focus a little bit and look at mathematics from another perspective. I think Plato would say that mathematics is a wonderful example of community. Here's what I mean by that apparently strange statement. Mathematics is the great equalizer. There's only one answer to a problem and it doesn't matter whether you are a man or a woman or young or old or from Greece or from Persia, from Athens, or from Sparta, the answer is the same. I think this gives, for Plato, a kind of inspiration about learning in general. He can imagine a common group of students who are working together towards the attainment of mathematical truth. They're bonded precisely by the common objective that they have, and because the objective is mathematical, it's there to be had by all.

It might be useful to reflect on this conception of education by contrasting it with some contemporary trends in education. There's a great deal of emphasis played in universities and high schools around the country on the notion of being inclusive. American educators are very concerned that certain ethnic groups might not feel included in, for example, higher education. There was a concern that women would feel excluded by certain forms of education. What, by and large, the typical American response to this need for inclusion has been is the answer, let's make sure that each of these individual groups gets their own little department in the university. So, when it comes to women we'll have women studies, and when it comes to African Americans we'll have African American studies, and if there are gay and lesbian people who want to be represented in the university, why not have a department of gay and lesbian studies; these are very common projects in American education.

I think Plato would find this backwards. Whether he's right or not is another question, and you certainly should think about that on your own. I think Plato would say, if you want to include African Americans and women and gays and lesbians, if you want to include everybody, let's have a common subject to aspire to. Let's have a universal truth towards which we aim that can embrace us all. Doesn't matter if you are a man or a woman, when you're solving a mathematical equation, you're on a level playing field and the answer will not be in the slightest bit prejudice.

Again, I'm offering these reflections to give you a general sense about Book VII. The details are very hard to follow concerning ancient mathematics, but the overall thrust of the chapter should now be making some sense. Especially when you remember our discussion of the Divided-Line, mathematics is fundamental in the formation of a philosophical soul, and our guardians must be philosophers so they can bring enlightenment into the city.

Here's a last way to put this point and to make a suggestion. If you've ever known a mathematician, it's likely this person will have told you that mathematics is beautiful. The greatest mathematicians have long felt this. They study mathematics not because it's practical, although it is, not because it's useful, but because the sheer beauty of formal structure, the sheer beauty of literally perfection, shines through in mathematical truth. To take a ridiculously simple example, the one I've cited, two plus two equals four is a perfectly true sentence. That has, as trivial as it is, a beauty to it. I think this notion of beauty has long inspired mathematically minded thinkers. I think it inspired Plato. As a result, in Plato's Academy, and you recall that was the school that he founded, mathematics seems to have been a prerequisite. One had to study geometry in order to enter Plato's Academy.

Let's turn to the culmination of the education of the guardians. Just as we learned in our study of the Divided-Line, it is called "dialectic." Socrates discusses this from 537b–541b. Dialectic is the study of forms. Dialectic is inspired by the "what is it" question that Socrates is famous for asking. The first and, perhaps, the most interesting point that Socrates makes about dialectic, is that it's potentially very dangerous, and it's especially dangerous for young people. As you read through Book VII, you'll see that the curriculum of the guardians is very rigidly regimented. Guardians, until they're about 20 years old, do very little else but engage in physical exercise and training. You'll recall that's called gymnastic. Between 20 and 30, these future rulers only study mathematics, but when they're 30 and up to about the age of 35, they start to get their first introduction to dialectic. To complete the sequence, between the ages of 35 and 50, the guardians will be required to go down into the cave where they will rule the city. Then, at the age of 50, they return to the study of dialectic, and only at that very late stage of their education will they finally get a peek at the Idea of the Good, the pinnacle of their study.

Now, I mention this point in conjunction with my earlier point that dialectic is potentially quite dangerous for young people. I want to elaborate a little bit on that. I told you a story several lectures ago that I'll repeat. Imagine that there is a young Athenian soldier, and his leaders tell him that he must go to war, and his leaders try to inspire him by telling him that this will be a just war. Perhaps, this was a soldier in the year 431 B.C.E. when the Peloponnesian War broke out. This soldier, in my hypothetical story, is on his way to serve in the army when he bumps into Socrates. What does Socrates do? He says, where you going, and the kid says, I'm going to war. Why are you going to war? Because the cause is just and I'm willing, even, to lose my life if my city requires me to do so. Socrates would then hit him with his question, what is justice?

Well, we have studied the *Republic*; we know how hard it is to answer this question. It's very difficult to imagine that a 19-year-old boy would be able to make any real progress in answering this question; he certainly wouldn't have an answer ready at hand. So he leaves the conversation with Socrates puzzled, confused, in a state of wonder, of bewilderment. What is justice? I thought I knew, I thought it was what my leaders told me was just, but this man Socrates has disrupted me. This man Socrates has taught me that I do not know what I thought I knew.

Well, what might happen? Maybe this boy will become a deserter, maybe he won't serve in the army or maybe even worse. Maybe this boy will say I don't know what justice is, maybe I'll go over to the Spartan side. Maybe they're just; maybe these Athenians who've been ordering me around aren't telling me the truth. Socrates has taught me that I don't know what justice is; the door is therefore open to me to do what ever it is I might want to do.

Now, I'm telling the story in this way because it corresponds to an actual event with an actual person. His name was Alcibiades, a very famous Athenian. He was famous for two things: he was an associate of Socrates and he was a traitor to Athens in the Peloponnesian War. He did, in fact, go over to the Spartan side. This, by the way, is no doubt one of the real reasons Socrates was executed in 399 B.C.E. He was thought to be associated with the traitor Alcibiades. The point I'm trying to make is that dialectical inquiry, the inquiry that begins with the question "what is it" and leads to an inquiry into the forms, is potentially subversive of the city. This is why in the educational program outlined in Book VII, Socrates does not allow young people to even be exposed to dialectic until they're at least 30 years old.

Let me tell another story that highlights this danger again. Plato wrote a dialogue titled the *Charmides*. In this dialogue, Socrates talks to a very promising, intelligent young man whose name is Charmides. Socrates asks him, what is moderation? Perhaps, you recall that moderation is one of the four great cardinal virtues. This boy is very famous for being moderate. His uncle, whose name is Critias, brags about him and says that Charmides is the most moderate, temperate, self-controlled boy I know. You can imagine what Socrates would do. He asks, what is moderation? Well, not surprisingly, Charmides doesn't know the answer to this question, nor does the older man Critias. At the end of this particular dialogue, we are left, as we so often are left with Socrates, with big fat question marks. We don't know what moderation is. In a similar fashion to my own hypothetical story about the young Athenian soldier who does not know what justice is. This dialogue titled the *Charmides* is one of Plato's most ingenious dialogues, because these two characters who are prominent in the *Charmides*, Charmides and Critias, later become two of the infamous thirty tyrants who appeared in 404 B.C.E., and whom we've discussed before. I think this is Plato's own way of reminding us of the dangers of dialectic, the dangers of philosophical inquiry. This is why the guardians are restricted to mathematical study for so long.

Plato's dialogues, including the *Republic*, are rather peculiar in this one sense. They are very often a study of failure. The *Charmides* is a prime example. Socrates fails to educate Charmides or Critias, he fails to turn Charmides around to use the metaphor developed in the parable of the cave, and he fails to turn Critias around. That's one kind of dialogue that we find very often.

There's a second kind of dialogue, and the *Republic* is an example. This is a dialogue where we readers, whether the reader was an Athenian or an American today, we readers, we don't know at the end of the *Republic* whether Socrates has succeeded with his main character, Glaucon. Has Socrates turned Glaucon to philosophy through his dialectical questioning, or has he perhaps subverted Glaucon, forced him to reconsider the traditional values he's always held, but not given him a real substitute. In short, dialectic is dangerous.

Let me close this lecture with a prefigurement of the next theme that we will study. With the education of the guardians completed at the end of Book VII, Socrates is now ready to face up to the question, is the just city possible? The construction project has lasted a very long time; it started in Book II, and it ends at the end of Book VII. Socrates is ambiguous. If you read the lines at 540b, you'll see Socrates saying, well I'm really not sure whether this just city that I've created in speech is possible or not. In fact, to quote directly from the text what he says is, "It's hard, but in a way, possible." That little phrase, in a way, signals the ambiguity.

There's one last thing we have to do if we want our city to become possible, says Socrates, and I'm referring now to 541a. This is the final condition of the possibility of the just city, and it's shocking. He says, "We must send everybody who is over the age of 10 out of the city." Now that is shocking, because when he says we must send them out of the city and into the country, what he must mean, to be blunt, is kill everybody over the age of 10. I think this is a fair inference, because you can certainly imagine if you were sending parents out of the city and keeping their children, these parents would immediately get together and say, let's go attack and get our children back. So to avoid that obvious eventuality, no doubt

Socrates is saying, if we want this city that we have taken such great pains to construct to come into existence, we're going to have to kill everybody over the age of 10.

In the next lecture we're going to discuss this proposal and use it as an occasion to raise a very big question about the *Republic* as a whole: does Plato take it seriously? Does he, in fact, think that everything he has discussed in the *Republic* is something like a blueprint for an actually just city? Or, perhaps, he doesn't take it as seriously as we might think.

Lecture Sixteen
Book VIII—The Perfectly Just City Fails

Scope:

As we move away from the third part of the *Republic*—the enormous philosophical detour of Books V–VII—and begin our return to the discussion of actual politics, we learn something surprising about Socrates's conception of the perfectly just city: It is doomed to fail. We discuss two reasons why. The first was mentioned in the previous lecture: In order for the perfectly just city to come into being, there must be a "clean slate"; thus, all citizens over the age of 10 will be removed from the city. This is monstrous, and Socrates could only have meant it ironically. What he is doing is showing that the perfectly just city is an impossible fiction, one that he himself would not wish to come into existence. Second, in order for the city to function properly, sexual relationships must be completely regulated by the rulers. Socrates explains that, in fact, this is impossible. The rulers fail to achieve the "marriage number," the scientific ability to control reproduction, or what today we would call *eugenics*. This lecture will explore the decline of the just city and prepare us for the next part of the *Republic*: an exploration of the "mistaken," the less-than-perfect regimes.

Outline

I. We begin where the last lecture ended: "all those in the city who happen to be older than ten" will be sent "to the country" (541a).

    A. Because the perfectly just city requires a comprehensive re-education of all citizens, it must begin with a "clean slate."

    B. Being "sent to the country" must mean "be killed."

    C. The perfectly just city is ruthlessly revolutionary.

        1. A comparison with Pol Pot's rule in Cambodia (1976–1979) is illuminating.

        2. Known as "Brother Number One," Pol Pot was responsible for the killing of between 1 and 3 million Cambodians. Children were often recruited to lead the revolution.

D. If Plato intends Socrates's proposal to be serious, then he is a monster on the order of a Pol Pot.

    1. Plato is not a monster.

    2. Therefore, he does not intend the proposal to be serious. He intends it as a demonstration of the absurdity of the perfectly just city.

    3. It is possible, therefore, that the *Republic* is a critique of political extremism.

    4. This is a controversial proposal, and students must form their own views on this matter.

II. The perfectly just city is not possible.

  A. Since the noble lie (414c), Socrates has stressed the importance of controlling sexual reproduction. The rulers must practice eugenics, making sure that gold-souled citizens mate with gold-souled citizens and raise gold-souled children.

  B. However, in Book VIII, we learn that the rulers fail to achieve a mathematically precise form of eugenics.

    1. They fail to discover the "marriage number" (546b–547a). As a result, there is "chaotic mixing" of bronze-, silver-, and gold-souled people.

    2. This passage is notoriously ambiguous, but it clearly symbolizes the inability of mathematics to capture and control what is essentially human: *eros*.

  C. *Eros* has been a hidden theme of the *Republic* since the beginning.

    1. In Book I, we learn that Cephalus is glad that the age of erotic madness has passed.

    2. Throughout the dialogue, we are reminded that Glaucon is erotic.

    3. In Book V, philosophy is characterized as the "love of the sight of truth." Philosophy itself, as the dialogues the *Symposium* and the *Phaedrus* teach, is an erotic activity.

  D. Mathematics, as we learned in Book VII, is crucial to philosophical education and is the paradigm of "science."

1. As powerful as it is, and as useful as it is in "turning around" the student from becoming to being, mathematics cannot do justice to the human soul.

2. Science cannot fully comprehend what it is to be human.

3. Therefore, there can be no such thing as a genuine philosopher-king who is able to govern a city of human beings with perfect knowledge.

E. The *Republic* is not a "blueprint."

1. It is a thorough examination of the human soul, which includes the love of and appreciation for mathematical truth.

2. The *Republic* demonstrates the beauty and value, but also the limitations, of mathematics.

III. The next stage of the dialogue (Books VIII–X) begins. Socrates discusses the "mistaken" regimes: the timocracy, the oligarchy, the democracy, and the tyranny.

A. The best regime is the aristocracy (rule by the best).

B. The second best regime (and first "mistaken" regime) is the timocracy, rule (*kratê*) by those who love honor (*timê*).

C. What is the genesis of the timocratic man (549c–550b)?

1. The father is the "aristocrat," the best of men. (*Aristos* means "best.") He is not concerned with money and power but with an ideal of excellence.

2. The mother is bitter that her husband doesn't have more money and power.

3. The son is drawn in two directions between his mother and his father (550a). He is in psychological conflict.

4. The son chooses a middle path: He becomes a lover of victory and honor.

D. The timocratic ruler seems to be like a Spartan.

E. The timocratic ruler is conflicted.

1. "Under cover of darkness he pays fierce honor to gold" (548a).

2. Because he is not fully educated, he cannot make a firm claim to virtue.

IV. The pattern is set for Books VIII and IX.

    A. Socrates discusses the four mistaken regimes and soul types.

    B. All are characterized by conflict and lack of education.

    C. All are deficient in their erotic attachments.

Essential Reading:

Plato's Republic, Book VIII.

Supplementary Reading:

Annas, J. *An Introduction to Plato's Republic*, pp. 297–298.

Roochnik, D. *Beautiful City: The Dialectical Character of Plato's Republic*, pp. 97–103.

Questions to Consider:

1. Socrates's "marriage number" seems to prefigure the contemporary science of genetic engineering. Do you think it would be reasonable and morally justifiable to try to "create" genetically superior human beings?

2. In a timocracy, great soldiers would become rulers. Do you think soldiers make for good political leaders? Why or why not?

Lecture Sixteen—Transcript
Book VIII—The Perfectly Just City Fails

I begin this lecture precisely where we left at the end of the previous lecture, with the very last proposal that Socrates makes in his enormous construction project of what he claims is a perfectly just city. This proposal is that everyone over the age of 10 be sent out of the city and into the country so that a clean slate can be established and a new regime can be constructed.

Socrates offers this proposal much like he offered the proposal, early in the *Republic*, that the family be abolished, and that men and women and children all be communally connected through the city. When he said those things in Book IV, he said them with a kind of casualness, as if he were making a minor change in public policy, whereas in fact, he was making an extraordinarily radical proposal. Glaucon and Adeimantus catch him on this at the beginning of Book V. This last proposal I just mentioned is uttered in the same tone of voice, as if it's a change in parking regulations, but in fact, as only a few seconds of reflection will convince you, it's a monstrous proposal. It's a monstrous proposal, but it contains within it, its own kind of logic. The *Republic* is supposed to be a revolutionary regime. It's going to come into being through a process, first and foremost, of education. It's very difficult to teach an old dog new tricks, and that's why Socrates recommends that everybody over the age of 10 to simply be exiled from the city.

Now, as I suggested at the end of the previous lecture, this is a euphemism. Socrates actually has in mind something much more drastic, because being sent to the country must be the same as killing them. Otherwise, unless these rulers are so silly that they can't predict this, the people who are sent into the country will get some weapons and come right back into the city to try to get their children back.

It might be useful to make a comparison here. I'm thinking of the vicious dictator of Cambodia who ruled from 1976–1979. His name was Pol Pot, and he was a tyrant and a murderer of the highest order. It's estimated that he killed somewhere between one and three million Cambodians. Now, I mention him because he seemed to have thought of himself as a revolutionary. He called himself "brother number one." Again, I mention that phrase because it seems to echo the themes that we have extracted from Plato's *Republic*. You recall the noble lie. The noble lie suggests that all citizens are brothers. The rulers would be first among equals, they would be brother number one. Pol Pot, in trying to wipe the slate clean so that a new world could be created, often put children into the vanguard of the revolutionary elite. It's a horrifying story, but it's also instructive. It teaches us something about the nature of revolutionary zeal.

When people like Pol Pot—perhaps people like Stalin—are so convinced that they know the absolute truth, that they understand how to move their country ahead, they might very well stop at nothing in order to bring their vision into reality. The most important thing they must do is to transform the population. This goes to the very essence of a revolution. If a revolution is going to succeed, the citizens must be fundamentally altered. They can have within them no vestiges of the old regime. Think also of the Cultural Revolution in China. The campaign was to reeducate all those citizens who still had within them some of the old ways. The new world was being born and, once again, the best representatives of the new world are children. What I'm proposing, in short, is that Socrates' monstrous suggestion at 541a, actually makes a very cold, cruel, but logical sense, if we think about the nature of genuine revolution.

I think we're faced with a dilemma in our reading of the *Republic*. There are two possibilities. If Socrates, and if Plato who is writing the dialogue, are serious about this last proposal to exile everyone over the age of 10, then we must put them in the same category as Pol Pot and Stalin. They're monsters. If Plato means this seriously, then Plato, in my view—and I hope in your view as well—should be despised. I would argue, however, that Plato is not a monster. Right now I must warn you that I'm going to offer you my own interpretation of this section of the *Republic* and indeed of the *Republic* as a whole. It's very important that you accept what I'm about to say in that spirit. There are many, many scholars who would disagree with me; some of them are represented in your bibliography. So I'm offering you the best shot I can give, but you yourselves should challenge me, because I want to make what in fact is a rather radical suggestion of my own, at this stage of our course.

I don't think that Plato intends this proposal at 541a in a serious manner. Indeed, I take it to be exactly the opposite. I think that the construction project that Socrates has engaged in from Book II until the end of Book VII that we are now studying, is what philosophers sometimes call a *reductio ad absurdum*, a reduction to absurdity. This is often the way that arguments are made. If I can demonstrate that a certain position leads to absurd consequences, then I have argued against the position. In an important sense, I think the so-called just city that Socrates constructs is absurd. I think Plato fully intends it to be absurd. He wants us, initially, and by us I mean the readers, he wants us initially to be chilled, to be disturbed by it. All along we've wondered, is Plato constructing a totalitarian regime in which sexual reproduction is rigorously regulated, in which people have no freedom, in which poetry is censored, and in which the education of the guardians is authoritarianly determined?

I would suggest to you, and I reiterate that this is only a suggestion, that this is all part of Plato's strategy. In other words, my interpretation of the *Republic* leads me to think that this dialogue is, in fact, a critique of political extremism. Plato understands—if I may speak anachronistically—people like Pol Pot; he understands what can happen when revolutionary zeal attempts to put itself into practice. What can happen? Precisely what Socrates proposes at 541a, everyone over the age of 10 is exterminated, so that there can be a clean slate and a brave new world can be constructed.

Take that with a grain of salt. Let me move to another angle on this same issue. The issue is, is the perfectly just city that Socrates proposes possible? This one is going to require far less interpretation on my part, because as you'll see, it's on the surface of the text. Socrates explicitly says what I'm about to describe.

Ever since the noble lie, which we encountered in Book III, Socrates has stressed the importance of what we have been calling eugenics, the control of sexual reproduction, and the attempt to create an excellent population. You recall from the noble lie that Socrates says the rulers must first and foremost keep control over the gold-souled people; gold-souled men must mate with gold-souled women. If by chance they give birth to a silver- or bronze-souled child, that child has to be taken away and put into its proper category; bronze-souled parents will raise bronze-souled children. It's a very horrifying vision that smacks of the sorts of 20th century, dystopic novels that we have discussed before; Orwell's *1984*, Huxley's *Brave New World*.

What happens at the beginning of Book VIII is extremely instructive in this regard, and I believe it supports my contention that, finally, Plato is criticizing much of what Socrates has constructed. At lines 546b–547a, we find an extremely obscure passage. Socrates goes to great lengths to describe what he calls the "marriage number." I won't attempt to decipher the mathematics. If you read it, I can promise you'll be puzzled by it, because it's very hard to make any sense of it. But this much we know, the marriage number, whatever actually it is mathematically, is an attempt to use mathematical science in the service of eugenics. Plato was a genius at predicting future intellectual developments. He understood, even though he didn't have the science available to him, that something like genetics, a science we now know so well, could be mathematically understood.

So the rulers of the so-called just city attempt to create a mathematical science of eugenics; this is the marriage number, and it fails. They fail. As a result of the failure, there is a chaotic mixing of bronze-, silver-, and gold-souled people. In short, mathematics cannot control *eros*, that all-important word in Plato's vocabulary. It's basic meaning is sexual desire, but it has much broader meanings as well. Again, I would argue that this explicit failure of the marriage number lends support to my general interpretation that, in fact, Plato's *Republic*, far from being a blueprint that future leaders should follow, is actually a critique of political extremism, a critique of revolutionary zeal.

Let me summarize some of the implications of this failure of the marriage number. I think it's instructive, because it brings into sharp focus, an intersection of two of the main themes that we've discussed since the beginning of this course. The first theme is mathematics, very much the focus of earlier lectures when we were discussing the education of the guardians and the Divided-Line.

The second theme is eros, and we have had eros in our view from the opening of the *Republic*. You recall, I hope, that scene in which the old man Cephalus says, I don't mind being old because my sexual desire has quieted. I am no longer tyrannized by eros. I'm peaceful. That's a peculiar scene if you read it simply in isolation from the rest of the *Republic*. Now that you've studied a good bit of the *Republic*, go back to that scene and it will richly echo later developments in the dialogue.

What we're learning in the marriage number failure scene, the beginning of Book VIII, is that Plato has been teaching us, for all these books, about this intersection of mathematics and eros. I would argue, in fact, that these are two of, if not the most, important— certainly among the most important—themes in the entire dialogue. To put the point as simply as I can, Plato believes that eros really constitutes the human soul. We are what we love. If we love food, we're food lovers; if we love political power, we're politicians. If we love beauty, perhaps we become artists. If we love wisdom, we're philosophers. To be human is to have strong desires to love, and that is definitive of who we are. This is a theme that is present in many of Plato's dialogues. You might take a look at the *Symposium*, *Phaedrus*, the *Lysis*; all of these dialogues concern, explicitly, the subject of eros. Most importantly, philosophy itself is an erotic activity.

Eros has been present from start to finish of the *Republic* in the person of Glaucon. We are told explicitly that he is an erotic man. It turns out that he seems to be bisexual; he has sexual desires for boys, sexual desires for girls. He's a thoroughly erotic man. It's precisely that fact that makes him into a potential philosopher. Cephalus, a man with no strong desires, can't be a philosopher. Glaucon may well become a philosopher, or he may not—the *Republic* may be yet another instance of Socratic failure, I mentioned this in the previous lecture—but he may. He has the potential energy to pursue the extraordinarily difficult tasks that philosophy demands of us. We have seen exactly what these tasks are.

Let me return you to the Divided-Line, and if you recall, I suggested to you at the time that the crucial move in the Divided-Line is to turn around, to resist the temptation of intellectual gravity. That's the moment when having achieved some knowledge of mathematics, we go back to the sensible world where mathematics proves to be so useful; instead, the true philosopher must resist that temptation, turn around, and move upwards. This requires energy. This requires passion. Glaucon has that.

Let me turn to mathematics. I've spent much of the previous couple of lectures explaining how important, how valuable, how good mathematics is to Plato. You'll recall that the study of mathematics, geometry in particular, was a prerequisite for getting into Plato's Academy, and I am not retracting any of those sentiments.

Mathematics is good, according to Plato, but it's not the best. Mathematics is in between. It's a very important subject to study, which is why it represents the bulk of the guardian's education in Book VII; however, it's not the ultimate form of intellectual inquiry, it can't capture what is essential to being human. In order to understand the human soul, some form of intellectual inquiry other than mathematics, and in fact, greater than mathematics, is required, and that's dialectic. That's philosophy as Socrates practices it.

So, to summarize one more time, Socrates has views that are very similar to our own. For us and for Socrates, good science, good useful technical knowledge, is mathematical. At the time he was writing, Plato was unaware of the extraordinary developments that of course we live with today, but the basic idea was already present even in ancient Athens. However, mathematical science can't get the job done completely, it can't capture what is essential to being human, this capacity for eros. As a result, there can be no real philosopher king or philosopher queen. Such a person would be the person who could mathematically engineer the population of the city. This, we discover explicitly at the beginning of Book VIII, is a failure, the failure of the marriage number.

With the failure of the marriage number, we have come to the end of the construction project. The *Republic* is structured very clearly. Book I is the prologue. Books II, III, and IV; Books V, VI, and VII; and then Books VIII, IX, and X, are three distinct sections, each of equal length. We have just completed that central section, V, VI, and VII; it's ended in failure. It might be interesting to turn back to the very beginning of that section, the very beginning of Book V. You'll recall that at the end of Book IV, Socrates says to Glaucon and Adeimantus, Plato's brothers, I'm done, I've created a just city, now it's my chance to tell you about unjust cities. At that point he is arrested. Of course, that was a playful metaphoric use of the notion of being arrested, but the young men around him say, wait a minute, Socrates, you can't do this, you can't go on to the next stage of the conversation. You have to explain to us this bizarre proposal you made that women and children and men will live in common and that there'll be no private sexual relationships.

That's an interruption, that's a trigger for what, in fact, is a digression, and the trigger is eros. So, Books V, VI, and VII, the central, the philosophical books of the *Republic* all constitute a very,

very long detour; a detour triggered by eros. Now that we have ended that stage, we're ready to resume the project that Socrates mentioned at the end of Book IV, and that is a discussion of the mistaken regimes. This constitutes the bulk of Books VII, IX, and X.

We are clearly on the descent; we are headed downwards. Using the language of the parable of the cave, we're headed back into the cave. We're headed away from the so-called perfectly just city, into the real world. The best regime, the so-called perfectly just city, could also be described as an aristocracy. This English word comes from two Greek words. The first, *aristos*, means excellent or best; the second comes from the Greek word *kratê*, which means power or rule. The aristocracy is rule by the best, rule by the excellent. In the case of the *Republic*, the aristocracy is not a matter of family lineage. To be an aristocrat is to be, of course, a philosopher, but as we have just learned at the beginning of Book VIII, the aristocracy fails. That's due to the failure of the marriage number.

As a result, we move to the second best regime. This regime is called the "timocracy." The suffix is the same, it comes from the Greek word *kratê*, power or rule; the prefix is from the Greek word *time*, which means honor. The timocracy is ruled by those who love honor, those who love victory. Socrates then launches into a description of the timocratic regime, as well as, the timocratic individual. This is a pattern that will be consistent for Books VIII and IX. Books VIII and IX you may think of as having four chapters. There are four mistaken regimes. These four regimes will be the timocracy, the oligarchy, the democracy, and finally, worst of all, the tyranny, and there'll be four corresponding personality types or character types. Of course these will be the timocrat, the oligarch, the democratic human being, and the tyrant. In each case, you'll find Socrates telling stories about how the individuals in this regime came about, whom they emerged from in the previous regime, and what they're like. Correspondingly we learn, of course, what the regime is like in which they are dominant.

So let's begin this process by taking a very quick look at the genesis of the timocratic man, this is found 549c–550b. This is the person who has a father who was an aristocrat, a member of that so-called perfectly just city. The father, because he was an aristocrat, was not concerned with money or power. We witnessed Socrates criticize those potential good things, and instead, replaced them by the love of real wisdom and real excellence. But the mother of this timocratic man is angry with her husband, because he doesn't have sufficient money or power. He spent all his time in the quest for this idealist excellence, and as a result, is impoverished and without real political power. The mother, says Socrates, is bitter and she puts pressure on her son.

What happens to the child? Common sense will tell you, and I'm referring now to line 550a, the son is conflicted. He's drawn in two directions; the father is advocating the pursuit of excellence, the mother is advocating the pursuit of money and power. What does the son do? He chooses a middle path. He becomes a lover of victory and honor. This is midway between the mother's desire, which is simply for money and power, and the father's idealistic desire for genuine excellence.

The timocratic ruler and the timocratic regime are pretty good, because the love of honor, Socrates says, is a very useful, regulating, and disciplining principle. If a ruler loves honor, they're not going to live in grand palaces, they're not going to exploit their citizens, and they're not going to boast about their wealth; they're concerned with the honors that the citizens themselves will confer upon them.

However, to repeat what will be the basic pattern of this entire section of the *Republic*, the timocratic ruler, as we've discussed, is conflicted. Socrates has a wonderful description of this person. At 548a he says, "under the cover of darkness he pays fierce honor to gold." The mother, you recall, is pressuring this boy to do better than the impoverished father, to make a lot of money, but the father is putting such pressure on the boy to care about excellence. So the boy comes up with a compromise: in public he is regulated by the love of honor, but as a result of all of his victories—his military victories, his political victories—he actually has amassed quite a fortune. But he won't allow himself to worship this fortune in public; only at night, when the doors are closed, will he gaze at his own wealth and really fall in love with it.

The pattern is now set for the rest of Books VIII and IX. We will repeatedly see such instances of psychological conflict and political strife.

Lecture Seventeen
Books VIII and IX—The Mistaken Regimes

Scope:

We begin by discussing the unusual quality of this, the fourth and final part of Plato's *Republic* (Books VIII–X). Unlike earlier sections, it is not a philosophical argument. Nor is it a historical analysis of how the political world actually works. Instead, Socrates tells an elaborate story of how regimes change. First, there is the aristocracy, the rule by the best (the *aristoi*), namely, the philosopher-rulers described in Books VI and VII. But, as we discussed in the previous lecture, this regime is doomed to fail. It becomes transformed into the timocracy, rule by the spirited few who excel in battle and achieve honor. In turn, this regime fails and becomes the oligarchy, rule by the wealthy few. Following this is the democracy, which then gives rise to the worst of all regimes, the tyranny. This lecture will review the timocracy, oligarchy, and the democracy.

Outline

I. Books VIII and IX of the *Republic* are rather peculiar.

    A. They do not contain philosophical arguments.

    B. They do not present a historical analysis.

    C. Instead, they comprise what is more like a story. Note that Socrates invokes the muse at 547a.

        1. Stories are often effective at communicating psychological insights.

        2. This will be the focus of our study of these passages.

II. Timocracy is rule by honor (547c–550c)

    A. The timocratic regime is ruled by those gripped by a love of honor.

    B. The timocratic individual is spirited, like Glaucon (548d).

        1. The timocrat is conflicted.

        2. In public, he values only public honor, but in private, he worships gold.

III. Oligarchy is rule by the wealthy few (550c–555b).

  A. The regime is ruled by the few (*oligoi*) who are rich.

    1. It is a divided regime: The rich rule and the poor are disenfranchised. They live within the confines of the same city but are always at odds with each other.

    2. It is a corrupt regime. "Virtue is in tension with wealth" (550e).

    3. It becomes a defenseless city: The rulers are afraid to arm the poor and do not want to spend the money to do so (551e).

    4. It is a "credit-card city": The rich have an interest in impoverishing the other citizens and, thus, are happy to extend them credit (552a).

  B. The individual citizen is like the regime.

    1. The son of the timocrat witnesses his honor-loving father lose all his money (553b).

    2. The son turns greedy and vows that this will never happen to him.

    3. He makes money the highest good. As such, he subordinates all of his other desires to his love of money.

    4. He becomes "a sort of squalid man" (554a).

    5. He neglects education.

    6. Money-love is paralyzing: At the prospect of actually spending some of his beloved money, "he trembles for his whole substance" (554d).

  C. Socrates is insightful about the psychological cost of money-love.

    1. He confirms the old saying "The more money you have, the more you worry about it."

    2. He carefully depicts how deadening money-love can be.

IV. Democracy is rule by the people (*dêmos*).

  A. It emerges from the oligarchy.

    1. The oligarchs are unwilling to discipline the youths who spend money because they become rich by encouraging the youth to spend freely (555c). Such young people become impoverished.

2. Sometimes, high-powered people are among the impoverished.

3. These people "sit idly in the city...hating and plotting against those who possess what belongs to them...gripped by a love of change" (555d).

4. A class of citizens emerges that revolts against the oligarchs.

5. The democracy comes into being.

B. Democracy is characterized by the following:

1. A democracy celebrates freedom (557b).

2. It protects the privacy (557b–557d) of its citizens.

3. It creates the conditions under which there can be diversity (557c).

4. It affirms the political equality (558c) of its citizens.

5. It has no rigid conception of a good life. As such, it is characterized by a kind of "formlessness."

Essential Reading:

Plato's Republic, Book VIII.

Supplementary Reading:

Popper, K. *The Open Society and Its Enemies*, pp. 45–68.

Roochnik, D. *Beautiful City: The Dialectical Character of Plato's Republic*, pp. 78–93.

Samons, L. *What's Wrong with Democracy?*

Questions to Consider:

1. Most Americans believe that democracy is the best of all possible regimes. Are they right?

2. Review Socrates's criticism of money-love and try to determine whether it is accurate. As much as possible, draw on your own experiences with money to address this issue.

Lecture Seventeen—Transcript
Books VIII and IX—The Mistaken Regimes

We've begun our descent into injustice. In other words, Socrates, in Book VIII, has begun his discussion of the unjust or the mistaken regimes. He always promised us that he would do two things, he would discuss both justice and injustice; in Book VIII he's fulfilling that promise.

We began our discussion in the previous lecture with a brief look at the timocracy, the best of the worst regimes. But before we continue, I'd like to take a step back and ask you to gain something of an overview of Books VIII and IX as a whole. The reason I suggest this is, in fact, that this section of the *Republic* is rather peculiar. It's peculiar because Books VIII and IX do not contain philosophical arguments. There's nothing resembling the sorts of arguments we've seen Socrates give in book I through Book VII. Nor do Books VIII and IX present us with historical information. We might expect them to do this because, after all, Books VIII and IX are a discussion of regimes such as the timocracy, which resemble—or apparently resemble—actual regimes such as Sparta. We will soon begin a discussion of democracy, and of course, we'll be immediately prompted to think about Athens.

Scholars agree, however, that Books VIII and IX don't do a very good job of accurately describing historical regimes. Nor do they suggest a real way of thinking about regime change, because much of Books VIII and IX are about just that, the timocracy gives way to the oligarchy, the oligarchy gives way to the democracy, and the democracy to the tyranny. This, once again, might appear to be almost a theory of historical change, of regime change, but it certainly can't be that; it's not sufficiently historical, nor is it accurate.

What, then, is it? That's a problem, and it has puzzled scholars. I want to make a suggestion to you: Books VIII and IX are like stories. My first piece of evidence to support this suggestion comes from 547a where you'll find Socrates, before he launches into his long account of regimes, invoking the muse. Invoking the muse is the standard opening of the epic poet. If you read Homer's *Odyssey* or *Iliad*, if you read Hesiod's *Theogony*, you'll see both poets beginning their storytelling by asking for assistance from the muse.

This is precisely what Socrates does. It's a very small bit of information, but useful, I think, in supporting this idea that what makes Books VIII and IX so strange is they have more of the quality of narrative, of storytelling, than of philosophical or historical argument.

We might stop now and ask ourselves, well why in the world would Socrates, the philosopher, start to tell us stories in Books VIII and IX? I think the answer to this question comes if we remember his basic strategy in Books VIII and IX. You recall that he will divide each section, each regime discussion, into two parts. The first will always be about the actual regime itself, the political organization of the timocracy, oligarchy, etc., but the second section—and I believe actually, the much more interesting section—will be a discussion of the individual who lives in that regime. So, we'll get a discussion of the timocracy and of the timocratic citizen, the oligarchy and the oligarch.

One of the things we know from all the stories we've read is that stories are a superb medium for communicating insight about character. We learn best about different kinds of individuals by reading stories about them, and this, I will suggest to you, is Socrates' reason for constructing this section of the *Republic* the way he does. His main purpose is to communicate something about certain kinds of human beings and the way he does so is through the telling of stories, and that's what I'll try to focus on in the next couple of lectures.

Let's very briefly review what we said about the timocracy, and this refers to lines 547c–550c. The timocracy, literally speaking, is ruled by honor. It's the form of government in which those who rule are those men who are gripped by love of victory, love of honor, love of glory. These are naturally men who are experts in warfare; these are men who are spirited, that all-important word that we initially encountered in Book II of the *Republic*. The timocracy is ruled by people like Glaucon, Socrates' conversation partner. If you look at 548d, you'll see an explicit mention of this fact.

What we learned about the timocracy and about the timocrat is that it's plagued by an essential kind of conflict. You remember that description that Socrates offers of the timocrat, he in his public life is dominated by a love of honor, but as a result of being so successful and so victorious in battle, he gains a lot of money. He's ashamed to, however, expose his love of money in public because he's so well known as a man of honor. But at night, in the dark, in his house, he worships gold; he worships money. He's a conflicted human being; his real desires, they come out at night, they can't be expressed during the day. This is a basic pattern that we'll see throughout Books VIII and IX. Both the regime and the individual are plagued with conflict.

You might contrast this with the basic model of justice that we have been discussing in earlier sections of the *Republic*. That model is best expressed metaphorically as a kind of harmony. You recall that there are, according to Socrates, three parts of the soul: reason, spirit, and desire, and that in a just individual, these three parts each do their own job. They work harmoniously; reason rules, and spirit is the ally of reason in its quest to subordinate desire.

What happens in each of the unjust individuals, as well as the unjust regimes, is that this nice harmonious working of different parts is out of whack. One part will dominate when it shouldn't, and in a timocracy, what's happening is that spirit is gaining power over the rest of the soul, and desire as well. That's exactly what is happening to the timocrat during the day. He is spirited, he loves victory, but at night, he gives into his desire for money. Eventually, and not surprisingly, this political system, as well as this individual, breaks apart; the conflict can't be sustained for too long. It's unstable.

What happens, again not surprisingly, is that the love of money, which the timocrat had only indulged at night in private, starts to take over his entire system and, therefore, the timocracy becomes the oligarchy. Oligarchy is rule by the wealthy few. The word *oligos* in Greek means "few," and specifically again, those few people who are very rich. It's discussed by Socrates in lines 550c–555b.

The essential problem with the oligarchy is that it creates an utterly divided city. On the one side are the rich, who rule, and on the other side are the poor, the majority of people who not only don't rule, but also, in fact, are disenfranchised. It is a very corrupt regime. At line 550e Socrates makes a pronouncement; he says, I quote, "virtue is intention with wealth." The desire for money, for wealth, is so powerful in people like the oligarch, that it overwhelms them and in fact obliterates their capacity to be good people, to be virtuous people, to be excellent people. You recall that the best regime was described as the aristocracy, ruled by the best, by the most excellent. We are two steps removed from the aristocracy when we encounter the oligarchy.

The rich and the poor live in the same city, but it's as if they live in two cities, so it's an utterly misleading sense of unity. You, perhaps, in your reading of this section of the *Republic* or even based only on my limited description of it so far, can, I hope, hear the real truth in what Socrates is describing. There were oligarchies in antiquity, and there are oligarchies all around the world today. In an oligarchy we find precisely what Socrates is describing; this mass of poor people who are disenfranchised and who are in the city, but out of the city at the same time. You might think of the giant mega cities like Mexico City where there are vast slums and these are filled with very poor people who have no real political role to play in the governance of their own city. The city, in an oligarchy, is run by this tiny cadre of very wealthy people.

The oligarchy is flawed, to say the least. For one thing, it rather quickly becomes a defenseless city. It can't defend itself against foreign enemies. This is for two reasons. First, the rulers are afraid to arm the poor people. They know that the poor people aren't very happy with their condition and they're quite fearful of giving them weapons because, obviously enough, they're scared that the poor people will use these weapons against them. That turns out to be a very legitimate fear on their part. Second, the rulers are just so stingy that they don't want to spend all the money it takes to equip a first-class army. I'm referring now, by the way, to 551e in your text. As a result of these fears, the oligarchy doesn't have a strong army; it's a sitting duck for its enemies.

There's another reason why the oligarchy is so flawed and such an inadequate regime, and here I'll speak anachronistically in order to try to bring this point to life in contemporary terms. I would describe the oligarchy as a credit-card city. Rich people have one thing in mind in the oligarchy, and that is to get richer. Well, how do you do that? One way is by extending credit to poor people. Let the poor people borrow, borrow, and borrow, charge exorbitant interest rates, and, if those poor people go broke, just take everything that belong to them. If you refer to 552a you'll see a description of just this dynamic, a familiar dynamic in contemporary life. I'm sure that you, like me, are bombarded in your mail slots with advertisements for credit cards. The banks want to sell credit cards. They want people to go into debt, because that's how a bank makes money. In an oligarchy, which is a vicious kind of wealth mongering, there is a ruthless expansion of credit, and then a ruthless reclaiming of the poor people's property. You can see the result, whether in terms of the inadequate army or in terms of an increasingly impoverished class of citizens, who are thoroughly disenfranchised, who will become thoroughly disillusioned with their own city; the oligarchy is doomed.

Let's turn next to the second chapter of the story about the oligarchy, and that would be a description of the oligarchic individual. You recall at the beginning of this lecture, I suggested that Plato is very, very interested in this side of each of his four chapters when he's discussing the four regimes. He's very interested in these kinds of personality types.

Plato is regularly thought to be a very otherworldly philosopher. That's not a bad characterization of Plato when we think of ideas like the forms, or the Idea of the Good, these eternal objects of intellectual contemplation. At the same time, however, I would urge you not to get too carried away with that description of Plato, because as you'll find in Books VIII and IX, he's also an astute observer of human psychology. Again, I suggested to you that this is perhaps why Books VIII and IX have this literary quality. They're storytelling in which character traits are revealed.

So let's engage in the story of the timocrat. As he did with the earlier section, Socrates begins with a history. The son of the timocrat witnesses his father, who is a lover of honor, losing all his money, and I'm referring here to 553b. Again, remember that the timocrat loves honor during the daytime, but loves money at night. As a result of this, the timocrat is not able to engage in moneymaking activities to the fullest extent possible during the day. He is too ashamed to do this. As a result of that, he doesn't make enough money. The son of the timocrat witnesses this and he turns greedy. He vows this will never happen to me, I'm going to make moneymaking my primary objective at night and during the day. It's a full-time job, making money. So he places money at the pinnacle of his list of desires. He becomes a money lover. This is where again I think Plato is so interesting, because Plato, I think, has a very accurate insight into the psychology of money love. He describes the oligarch, the person who emerges from the timocrat as, and I'm quoting from 554a, "a sort of squalid man," a dried-up man, a man who is inhibited in the most basic sense.

This is a person, the oligarch, who neglects everything—including education, which as we know from our study of Plato, is paramount—in service of his quest to earn more and more money. But there is in money love a very basic paradox. Somebody who wants a lot of money, who loves money, will spend all of his energy trying to get it; that makes sense. But there's a very big problem here, it's a problem that we encounter in the real world all the time. Somebody who has a lot of money loves money; but money has no value by itself. If I simply sit home at night and worship my hundred dollar bills, it's worthless. Money is only useful when it's spent. But the true money lover, who has devoted so much energy to accumulating a fortune, can't spend money. They are incapable of giving away what they worked so hard to get. So Socrates describes this in a very, I think, poignant way, at 554d. At the prospect of spending money, the oligarchical human being, the money lover, I quote, "trembles for his whole substance."

Another way to put this point is to cite an old cliché almost, which is "the more money you have, the more you worry about it." Money can become a consuming passion. People regularly think that money is going to make them happy—"If only I had more and more money, then I'd finally be free from all the worries I now feel, because I'm so worried about paying my bills and sending my kids to college, etc." It doesn't work that way. When people receive a lot of money, for example—and you've read these stories in the newspapers, when someone unexpectedly wins millions in the lottery—very frequently their whole life is disrupted. Their whole life is, to their immense surprise, made miserable. Why is it made miserable? For all the reasons that I think Socrates so interestingly dissects in this section of the *Republic*. The more money you have, the more you want it, the more you worry about it; to have money is often nothing but a trigger to wanting even more money. In short, the love of money is potentially paralyzing. Paralyzing in the sense of paralyzing your desires, or all your desires except for that one rather squalid desire, which is the desire for ever more money.

I'll tell you one story that I think substantiates this point, and perhaps you know stories that are similar. I had a friend who was a lawyer and one of his jobs was, frequently, to settle the estate of farmers. Often he would encounter a farmer who had died. He would go to the person's house; it would be a house in terrible condition. He'd find that the farmer had been living in near poverty, and then, literally, under the mattress, he would find hundreds of thousands of dollars. The farmer had been caught in just the psychological trap that Socrates so insightfully dissects in this section of the *Republic*. We can see, then, in terms of both the regime and the individual, the oligarchy is doomed. It is fundamentally unstable and the oligarch is a deeply flawed individual.

We move next, perhaps not surprisingly, to democracy. This word means in the original Greek, rule by the people, the *dêmos*. The democracy emerges from the oligarchy and you can, I think, predict why. The oligarchy has so thoroughly disenfranchised large numbers of very poor people and these people are increasingly dissatisfied with their lot in life. They want to participate in their own city; you recall that description of the oligarchy as being really two cities in one. The oligarchs are unwilling to discipline their own young people. This is another reason why the oligarchy is doomed to fail. Oligarchs have no interest in education; they have no interest in anything except making money. What we have learned from earlier stages of the *Republic* is that education is really the way to teach people how to act properly, to discipline their desires, but there is no investment in education in the oligarchy. So we have a whole cadre of very young people who, because they have been seduced into using credit cards—of course I'm speaking anachronistically; in other words, going into heavy debt—they are now impoverished. Some of these young people were formerly middle-class or even wealthy. It doesn't matter to the oligarch; as long as the oligarch continues to make money, he doesn't care who it is that becomes impoverished.

These become people who are very dangerous to the regime, because these are not worthless people; these were formerly middle-class or wealthy people, and now what's happening? I'll refer you to 555d. These become people who sit idly in the city hating and plotting against those who possess what belongs to them, gripped by a love of change. The key line there would be, "hating those who possess what belongs to them." These are kids who have had all their possessions reclaimed by the banks, by the oligarchs. They become revolutionaries; they love change, and they overthrow the oligarchy, ruled by the rich, and they replace it with what initially is ruled by the poor, by the majority who are poor, and this is the inception of the democracy.

We'll close this lecture with a preliminary look at Socrates' discussion of democracy. I should warn you in advance that it will be extremely controversial, because Socrates will be extremely critical of democracy. We will devote all of the next lecture to this one question of Socrates' critique of democracy. This next lecture will be among the most important we will have in this entire course, because democracy plays such a pivotal role in our own political lives. It's very dear to us, and in the next lecture in particular, we will see what reasons there possibly could be to criticize it. At this point, though, let's just look at some of the basic features of the democracy that Socrates discusses.

First and foremost, I'm referring to 557b, "a democracy celebrates freedom." Freedom of speech, freedom of religion, freedom of expression, all of these freedoms that we Americans hold so dear were also held dear by the Athenians. You recall that Athens had a democracy for at least a hundred years; all of the 5th century except for the very end, 404 B.C.E., when it was toppled by the tyranny for a very short time. Another very basic feature of democracy as Socrates describes it—and this will again ring perfectly true to us, a very familiar notion—it protects privacy. I would refer you to lines 557b–d.

The way you might want to frame this discussion of privacy is to remind yourselves of something that Socrates says when he was discussing the famous parable of the cave. You recall, perhaps, that the prisoner is liberated and brought out to the sun, in other words, engages in philosophical contemplation, but then is forced to go back into the city into order to rule. In Socrates' regime, the so-called justice regime, there is no option but to be political. In a democracy, then and now, there is no compulsion to be political. If an American citizen wishes to participate not at all, he or she is free to do that. There's no law that even forces us to vote. So we are perfectly welcome in our country and in the democracy Socrates is describing in the *Republic*, to lead private lives.

As a result of these two conditions, the protection of freedom, indeed the celebration of freedom, and the protection of privacy, diversity is a feature of a democracy. Look at 557c and you'll see Socrates' description of the diversity in a democracy. Precisely because people are free to lead their own private lives, because they're free to pursue their private projects, perhaps they want to be artists, perhaps they want to be athletes, perhaps they want to be musicians. It's up to them; they're free to choose. We have a wide variety of different kinds of human beings in a democracy. Again, true today and true in Plato's *Republic*.

Another feature of democracy is equality, equality before the law. I would refer you to 558c. All citizens, regardless of their financial stature, regardless of their physical or intellectual stature, are all considered to be equal before the law. As a result of these four qualities of a democracy, Socrates will argue, and we'll explore this argument in some depth in the next lecture, that democracy is a kind of formlessness. It has no definite shape; there is no rigid conception of a good life, there is no rigid conception of how one ought to speak, what sort of art, what sort of music one ought to pursue and, as a result, from Socrates' perspective, the result will be very close to chaos, or again, the formlessness. And that will be the theme of our next lecture.

Lecture Eighteen
Book VIII—Socrates's Critique of Democracy

Scope:

This lecture elaborates on the themes of the previous one. We explore in some depth Socrates's criticisms of democracy, and we counter them with various arguments on behalf of democracy. This lecture, therefore, addresses what is perhaps the most politically charged issue found in this course. We live in a democracy and, thus, we tend to affirm it unconditionally. Socrates's challenge may be uncomfortable, but responding to it should sharpen students' understanding of the regime that they likely think best.

We conclude with a discussion of this passage: "It is probably necessary for the man who wishes to organize a city, as we were just doing, to go to a city under a democracy" (557d). This is most surprising (and typically Platonic): After apparently condemning democracy in the most hostile of terms, Socrates seems to suggest that the very activity taking place in the *Republic* itself would "probably" occur only in a democracy.

Outline

I. The democratic individual comes into being in the following way.

   A. The oligarch is unwilling to invest in his son's education (559d). Thus, the son is undisciplined and vulnerable to the lures of the "unnecessary desires" (558d). He becomes a democrat.

   B. The democratic individual is whimsical. He has no stable character, because he has not been properly educated (561c–d).

   C. He is hostile to all forms of authority (563d).

      1. A democracy becomes a "youth culture" (562e–563a).

      2. A democracy is "formless" (563c).

II. There are similarities between the democracy Socrates condemns and the democratic America in which we live.

    A. Do we live in a youth culture?

    B. Are we excessively egalitarian?

    C. Are we formless?

    D. Is there too much freedom?

III. Socrates is finally ambivalent toward democracy.

    A. He says, "it is probably the fairest of all regimes" (557c).

    B. Most surprisingly, he also says, "It is probably necessary for the man who wishes to organize a city, as we were just doing, to go to a city under a democracy" (557d).

        1. This seems to imply that only in a democracy is the sort of philosophizing found in the *Republic* possible.

        2. Perhaps the freedom of speech and the protection of privacy available in a democracy are conditions that allow philosophy to flourish.

        3. Recall the ship of state parable discussed in Lecture XI. Perhaps a philosopher in a real city leads a private, not a political, life.

IV. The culminating criticism of a democracy is that it leads to tyranny.

    A. The democracy is "drunk" (502d) with the concept of freedom.

    B. Therefore, the rulers must flatter, rather than educate, the citizens.

    C. A demagogue, the supreme flatterer, emerges (565c). He eventually gets control of the entire city.

Essential Reading:

Plato's Republic, Book VIII.

Supplementary Reading:

Monoson, S. *Plato's Democratic Entanglements*, pp. 5–29.

Popper, K. *The Open Society and Its Enemies*, pp. 45–68.

Roochnik, D. *Beautiful City: The Dialectical Character of Plato's Republic*, pp. 78–93.

Samons, L. *What's Wrong with Democracy?*

Questions to Consider:

1. Is Plato, as Karl Popper thought, an enemy of the "open society"?

2. Socrates seems to characterize the democracy as a "youth culture," in which all authority, including that of parents and teachers, is despised. Does this seem true of American democracy?

Lecture Eighteen—Transcript
Book VIII—Socrates's Critique of Democracy

We continue our discussion of Socrates' critique of democracy. No regime is more dear to us than a democracy, no regime was more dear to the Athenians, nonetheless, Socrates will prove to be a ruthless critic of it. Just to very briefly review, you recall that democracy emerges from the oligarchy. The oligarchy had disenfranchised the majority of its own citizens, the poor. The poor rise up in revolt, and easily topple the oligarchs, because, after all, the oligarchs were unwilling to invest in a good army. The democracy is established, it has at least four basic qualities, and it affirms freedom, privacy, equality, and diversity.

Let's focus next on the democratic individual, always the two-part chapter system that Socrates uses to discuss each of the four kinds of unjust regimes. Who is this individual? He is the son of the oligarch. Perhaps, to get a picture of the sort of story that Socrates is telling, let's conjure up a scene; let's imagine dinner at the oligarch's house. The son is sitting there with the father. The father has only one thing to say over dinner, "Don't spend money. Be frugal, all those things that you want, you really shouldn't want; instead, you should devote yourself to the same pursuit I've devoted myself, namely, the pursuit of money." The son, of course, knows that his father's very rich, so there is a very basic discord, or disconnect, between what the father is saying and what the father has actually practiced. The father is unwilling to invest in education, his only objective, as we discussed in the previous lecture, is to make more and more money. He is unwilling to invest even in the education of his own son. As a result of this, the son is very undisciplined; he is intoxicated with what Socrates, at line 558d, calls "unnecessary desires."

A necessary desire, for example, would be the desire for drink when you're thirsty, the desire for food when you're hungry. We have to act on these desires, or we will cease to exist. Unnecessary desires offer things we don't absolutely need. Perhaps you recall the basic transition that was pivotal in Book II when we had the transition between the first original city, which only met the basic needs of its citizens, and the second city, the city that is sparked by Glaucon's objection, the city of unnecessary desires. It includes perfume, courtesans, art, and so many other luxuries that are very much echoed in this section of the *Republic*. The son of the oligarch, the rich, stingy old man, is wild at heart, because he was deprived of every sort of pleasure, even though his father could provide it because his father is so rich. So what does this kid do after dinner? He goes out into the city, out onto the streets, and there he's exposed to all sorts of chaos, all kinds of desires, all kinds of pleasures, and he becomes enthralled by them. This is the genesis, the coming into being, of the democratic individual.

Socrates, in lines 561c–d, gives a very elaborate description of this individual, and I would urge you to read that passage very carefully. What you'll find is that, above all else, the democratic individual is whimsical. He has no stable character. We know why, he hasn't been properly educated. In this passage Socrates describes such a person as sometimes he exercises when he feels like it, other times he overeats, sometimes he drinks a lot, other times he doesn't. Sometimes he participates in politics. For example, if he hears a great speaker, he might become very enthusiastic about that candidate. If he hears somebody on the streets saying our country must go to war, perhaps this kid will even join the army; he's very much subject to whims. Sometimes—and this is the remarkable injection in this passage and I will return to it near the end of this lecture—sometimes, this democratic individual even engages in philosophy. Perhaps the kid bumps into Socrates on the street, gets interested in one of these famous "what is it" conversations, and for a short time becomes interested in philosophy. Until, of course, something else captures his fancy and he shifts focus yet again.

Above all else, this young person, the democratic individual, is hostile to all forms of authority. We know why. The paramount value of a democracy is the affirmation of freedom. An authority of any form seems to threaten our freedom. I'm reminded of a license plate I have often seen; perhaps you have as well, a license plate of New Hampshire. On it, it says, "Live free or die." I'd rather be dead than to submit to authority. This would be the Socratic interpretation of that license plate.

What I would suggest to you, and here I'm offering you an interpretation of lines 562e–563a, is that a democracy becomes what I would call, a "youth culture." Precisely because it's hostile to authority, it's hostile to traditions. There's no sense of the goodness of being an elder. In fact, it's exactly the opposite. In a democracy where freedom has such overwhelming value, any notion of an elder, a traditional authority, is unwelcome. Socrates gives several examples of this. One of them is, in a democracy, he says, teachers start to fear their students. Students are so rambunctious, they're so undisciplined, and so hostile to authority, that they actually can threaten teachers. If this sounds familiar as a commentary about our own democracy, I think that's a useful thought. Parents, in a democracy, have a very difficult time disciplining their own children, and if the children are obstinate enough, they may simply give up and say the heck with it, you go out there, do what you want. Again, all of this derives from the fact that in a democracy, freedom has such enormous value.

So let me now raise very explicitly the question, whether the democracy Socrates is describing is, in fact, similar to our own democracy. I'm going to do this in the hope of provoking you to reflect upon something that's very dear to all of us, our very own political system. We accept it as good. The Socratic, the philosophical demand, always regardless of what your views are, is not to simply accept traditional or conventional wisdom, but to challenge it, to think for yourself. This is a very good occasion for us to do that. So I'm going to take a Socratic position myself and offer you a criticism of contemporary American society that is parallel to the criticism Socrates offers.

I would argue that, just as Socrates says, our own democracy has indeed become a youth culture. Obvious examples of this: think of our sense of fashion. The image of a young person is so utterly dominant in our media—everyone wants to look young. They want to look thin; they hate the idea of having wrinkles. Nothing is worse than looking old, and people in our time are willing to go to extraordinary lengths, in terms of surgery, injection of drugs, anything it takes. Nothing could be worse than looking old, nothing could be worse than being old. In itself, this is perhaps not such a significant phenomenon; however, I think it, in fact, is very interesting as confirmation of what Socrates is suggesting is basic to a democracy. There is just such distaste for authority and tradition, that there's no reason, no compelling reason, to simply value the old, only because they're old. In fact, it's exactly the opposite. I would hesitate to guess how many billions of dollars are spent by the pharmaceutical industry in keeping people looking young.

Another example of our own society that confirms Socrates' diagnosis is one I mentioned earlier; the discipline in schools. There are many schools in our country where teachers are quite literally afraid of their own students. There are many schools in this country where students have to walk through a metal detector before they enter to make sure that they don't carry weapons. I work at a university; I don't face that sort of danger, I'm happy to say. But there is something that I do face, which is once again reminiscent of something Socrates says. Every semester at a university, my students fill out evaluations of the course. In some universities and some colleges, these evaluations are taken to be critical in determining the value of the professor. In some colleges, a professor will not be rehired if he or she doesn't get good student evaluations. I think if Socrates were to observe this going in our colleges and universities, he would be utterly appalled, because what will happen? Well, the teacher will become afraid of the student. Nothing could be worse than offending our students. Nothing could be worse than making the class really hard and perhaps even a bit painful, because after all, the teacher might get bad student evaluations.

I once worked in a college where a colleague of mine told me her strategy for getting good student evaluations. She said she would always make sure the day before she was going to distribute the student evaluations, she would serve cookies. Now, this is, I think, a very backwards sense of what the teaching enterprise really is. I'd refer you back to the parable of the cave. One point I emphasized more than once was the fact that this image of our education, and that's what the parable of the cave is said to be, implies a great deal of pain. The prisoner at the bottom of the cave is shackled and must be liberated. This is very painful, because the prisoner has been sitting very long. The prisoner must look at the fire, the prisoner eventually must look at the sun, and this is very painful because the prisoner has been in darkness and it will literally hurt his or her eyes to be exposed to such bright light.

I suggested to you in our interpretation of the parable of the cave, that what this pain reflects is the difficulty of education. Students have to be pushed hard in order to challenge conventional wisdom, in order to think for themselves. Precisely that notion of hard discipline, Socrates says, is missing in a democracy for all the reasons we've outlined.

Let me raise another question. Socrates criticizes democracy for being excessively egalitarian. An egalitarian is someone who believes that human beings are equal. Perhaps you're thinking, what in the world could be wrong with that idea, aren't people equal? Isn't that taken to be a self-evident truth in our own society?

Well, I'll to try to elaborate Socrates' critique of excessive egalitarianism; I'll take you back to an earlier issue we discussed. Perhaps you recall the lecture that concerned Socrates' medical ethics. It was a very severe form of medical ethics. Socrates has a basic principle, which is if somebody is wounded, or if an otherwise healthy person gets a cold, yes, they should be treated. But if somebody is chronically ill and has no hope of being restored to a healthy productive life, they simply should be let go. What I would suggest to you is that sort of medical ethics, Socrates', is not egalitarian. It's making a basic value distinction in kinds of human beings. Some human beings are more valuable than others. Some human beings deserve medical treatment, they deserve the use of our medical resources, but others do not. I gave the example in that lecture of a 90-year-old man who's suffering from Alzheimer's. Socrates would say, and this is shocking, I think, to our ears, Socrates would say such a person is just not equal to a 30-year old man who's physically and mentally strong. If we must take the medical support system away from such a man, in fact, that's a rational decision.

To go back to the critique that I would extract from Book VIII of the *Republic* and apply to contemporary American society, to go back to imitating Socrates, our own system of medicine is a thoroughly egalitarian one. A doctor in a hospital operates with one imperative, keep the patient alive. It doesn't matter if the patient is a 90-year-old man suffering from Alzheimer's, or a 30-year-old man who's otherwise healthy. The objective is always the same; life and then more life; all life is good. There is no distinction between life and a good life. This was the theme of the earlier lecture concerning medical ethics.

That's precisely what Socrates means in Book VIII by "excessive egalitarianism." All human beings, he believes, are not equal. Some are worse than others. A very challenging thought, to say the least. I certainly wouldn't encourage you to simply accept it, in fact, the opposite. Challenge it; think about it. To continue, Socrates believes that democracy is formless, it's chaotic, there is no stable conception that somehow regulates us all and gives us a sense of what is a good life. That is what he means by chaos. There is, in short, too much freedom. Especially young people should not be allowed simply to maximize their own options. They should be, to put it very bluntly, told what to do; this is the Socratic view.

So, if we put all of these criticisms together, I think you'll find the heart and soul of the Socratic critique of democracy. It's one of the most famous; in fact, I would think the most famous criticism of democracy that can be found in the history of western political philosophy. It has gotten many, many people angry.

Now, let me say something that, in fact, is very surprising. I don't think most readers or scholars pay nearly enough attention to it in their understanding of the *Republic*. Socrates, despite these severe criticisms of democracy that he makes, is actually ambivalent when it comes to democracy. Let me give you two quotes. The first is from 557c. He says, "It is probably the fairest, the most beautiful of all regimes." Even more surprisingly, he says the following at 557d, "It is probably necessary for the man who wishes to organize a city, as we were just doing, to go to a city under a democracy." That line is surely worth rereading. Because what Socrates in effect is saying, is that if we want to do what we are right now doing, then maybe we have to be in a democracy. Well, what are we right now doing? "We" here refers to Socrates and Glaucon and Adeimantus, but also us, the readers. What we are right now doing is engaging in philosophy. So Socrates, at 557d, comes very close to saying, perhaps it's only in a democracy that we can practice philosophy.

We've had some clues about this possibility in earlier stages of the *Republic*, and let me remind you of what they are. First of all, when I was describing the democratic individual, who I said was whimsical, I mentioned that Socrates says that this person sometimes exercises, sometimes drinks a lot, and sometimes engages in philosophy. Now, that engagement with philosophy is very short-lived and not very substantial, but it is, nonetheless, a mention that the democratic person might engage in philosophy.

Another example, I've mentioned that a basic feature of democracy is the protection of privacy. What this means is there is no obligation, no compulsion, to be political. This is quite different; in fact, it's the opposite of what we find in the parable of the cave where the philosopher has to be returned to the cave, has to be forced back into the cave; in other words, forced to be political. This is mimicked in the very beginning of the *Republic*. You recall Socrates is on his way home and he's forced, playfully, to stay in the Piraeus. The notion here would be in a democracy, where privacy is guaranteed, a person could pursue philosophy precisely because they don't have to be political.

Another point, and again, this is a point I don't think most readers or scholars pay quite enough attention to—I tried to suggest it in my early lectures—where is the *Republic* set? It's set in the Piraeus. What was the Piraeus? It was the stronghold of democratic opposition to the Tyranny of the Thirty in the years 404 and 403 B.C.E. One of the main characters in Book I of the *Republic* was Polemarchus. What do we know about him historically? He was executed by the tyrants. He was a democracy fighter. All of these clues lead me to wonder whether, in fact, Socrates' criticism of democracy isn't quite as blunt and hard-edged as it's very often taken to be.

I'll put this point in one other way as a means of summarizing. Perhaps freedom of speech and the protection of privacy are necessary conditions for the possibility of philosophy. Isn't this what we imagine philosophy to be? If you and I are engaged in a philosophical conversation, what we want, above all else, is to be able to follow that conversation wherever it may lead. We don't want to be hemmed in intellectually at all. We want to be given the chance to talk all night if we want to. If you measure the length of the *Republic*, it's a very long dialogue; it has ten books. It's one conversation. These people were apparently talking all night. Where were they talking? In a private home, the home of Cephalus and Polemarchus. I think the setting, again, is meaningful. This conversation that we have been engaged in from the very beginning, itself takes place under the conditions available in a democracy.

Don't misunderstand me; I'm not suggesting to you that Socrates' criticisms of the democracy were not serious. I think he meant each and every one of them. Democracy is excessively egalitarian, there's too much freedom, there's chaos, and it's very often a big mess; the notion of formlessness that I introduced. Nonetheless, perhaps what Plato is finally trying to teach us about democracy, is a very old lesson that's been echoed through the centuries. As bad as it is, and it is bad, it's the best available. I've already suggested to you—and this was my interpretation, I warned you of this at the time, I urge you to take my interpretation with a grain of salt—I've suggested that the edifice of the just city—which, if you recall, culminates in the expulsion of every citizen over the age of 10, that comes from the end of Book VII—is meant to be a demonstration that excessive authoritarian justice is actually not desirable. I used the phrase *reductio ad absurdum*. I'm not sure at all that Plato is serious about constructing a just city and thinking it to be really the best city that we should all actually aspire to.

In other words, I reject what you might call the "blueprint theory" of Plato's *Republic*. The blueprint theory is the notion that what we find in Books II through VII is a blueprint for an actual regime that we should aspire to. That is what I'm challenging, that's exactly parallel to what I'm suggesting here about Socrates' criticism of democracy. On the one hand, he means it; on the other hand, it's possible that there are certain hidden virtues in a democracy that he, in fact, is willing to affirm. The primary virtue would be the possibility of philosophy itself. After all, Socrates, the historical figure, lived from 469–399 B.C.E. Plato lived from 427–354 B.C.E. They lived in Athens. Athens was a democracy. So, they flourished. Now, of course they didn't simply flourish, because Socrates was executed in 399 B.C.E. and Plato was undoubtedly overwhelmed by this experience in 399 B.C.E. I think if we put these two ideas together, we come up with this notion that, finally, Plato is ambivalent about democracy. It has terrible faults, one of them being the fact that the Athenian democracy executed Socrates, but it also allowed for Socrates in the first place.

Let me conclude this lecture with what turns out to be the culminating criticism of democracy. That is, according to Socrates, that a democracy leads to tyranny and here's why. The democracy, he says at 502, is "drunk" with the concept of freedom. As a result of this, the rulers must do what? We've already discussed this. The citizens are so hostile to any form of authority that rulers must flatter the citizens; they must please the citizens, in much the same way that a teacher must entertain the students. So the ruler must entertain, please, and satisfy the desires of the citizens.

As a result of this dynamic, what emerges from a democracy, says Socrates, is the demagogue. The word demagogue comes from the Greek word *dêmos*, same as democracy, and the last part of that word means leader. The demagogue is the leader of the people. He is the supreme flatterer. He is the ultimate populist. He captivates the imagination of the majority of the citizens and becomes first among equals. Eventually, this person becomes a tyrant and as we will find in the next lecture, there is no regime worse than the tyranny.

Lecture Nineteen
Books VIII and IX—The Critique of Tyranny

Scope:

Socrates offers a lengthy discussion, and thorough condemnation, of tyranny, the worst of all possible regimes. We will discuss how the tyrant emerges from the democracy, how he gets power, and what, finally, makes his rule so morally and politically bankrupt. Despite his feelings of omnipotence, the tyrant is actually the unhappiest and most slavish of men. This section of the dialogue contains a penetrating analysis of the effect power has on people. We will test Socrates's analysis by comparing what he says to what is known about the most notorious tyrant of our generation: Saddam Hussein.

Outline

I. The demagogue becomes the tyrant.

    A. The demagogue poses as the champion of the people, especially the poor (565a–c).

        1. He demands his own bodyguards (566b).

        2. He gets a taste of blood by executing those of the rich who hate the poor (566c).

        3. Intoxicated by his own power, he expands his power base. He promises the poor "freedom from debts" and to "distribute land to the people" (566e).

    B. The tyrant instigates war against other cities so that his people will need a strong leader—so that they will need him.

    C. He begins to execute those among his former allies who have "free thoughts" (567a). They represent potential threats to his rule.

        1. The tyrant has no friends. Only sycophants surround him.

        2. Both he and his regime are impoverished by his desire to stay in power. The tyrant spends lavishly (568d).

        3. The tyrant is willing to kill his own father to retain power (569b).

D. The tyrant is a slave to his passions. He is willing to act on those savage impulses (572b) —desires that lie in the hearts of all men.

E. The tyrant is always at risk of assassination, unable to travel freely.

II. The accuracy of Socrates's depiction of the tyrant can be seen in reflecting on the career of Saddam Hussein.

    A. Plato was personally familiar with tyranny; recall the Tyranny of the Thirty of 404.

    B. Saddam Hussein is a gripping example of a contemporary tyrant.

        1. He joined the Baath Socialist Party in 1956. As Socrates says, he began as a champion of the poor.

        2. By 1979, he was the president of Iraq.

        3. He initiated and prolonged an eight-year war against Iran from 1979–1988. As Socrates says, it is in the interest of the tyrant to keep his city at war.

        4. It has been said that "Saddam is a dictator who is ready to sacrifice his country, just so long as he can remain on his throne in Baghdad" (BBC News, Middle East Web site).

        5. He brutalized his own population. He used chemical weapons against the Kurds.

        6. He executed many of his own generals, and as a result, his army was less proficient than it could have been.

        7. As Socrates says, he was unable to travel freely. He had many palaces and constantly feared assassination (579d–e).

        8. He allowed no criticism and, hence, was surrounded by sycophants.

        9. He led his country to disaster. As Socrates says, "there is no city more wretched than one under a tyranny" (576e).

III. There is a surprising and uncomfortable similarity between the philosopher and the tyrant.

    A. Both are erotic. The tyrant has a passionate love of power, and the philosopher has a passionate love of wisdom. In fact, "love has from old been called a tyrant" (573b).

    B. The theme of *eros* runs through the *Republic* from the very first scene. Plato witnessed tyranny firsthand; it is not surprising that this theme is so prevalent in the *Republic*.

    C. Both the tyrant and the philosopher have a disregard for convention.

    D. Both are bullies in their own way.

    E. There are two kinds of tyrant: private and public (578c). Who would be the private tyrant? The answer is, someone who is dominated by his interests, such as a philosopher who is dominated by his love of wisdom.

Essential Reading:

Plato's Republic, Books VIII and IX.

Supplementary Reading:

Roochnik, D. *Beautiful City: The Dialectical Character of Plato's Republic*, pp. 86–93.

Questions to Consider:

1. Have there been any American demagogues who threatened to become tyrants? You might want to consider the case of Huey Long.

2. Do you agree with Socrates when he says that love is a tyrant? What does this mean?

Lecture Nineteen—Transcript
Books VIII and IX—The Critique of Tyranny

At the end of the last lecture we were witnessing the emergence of the demagogue. The demagogue is the leader of the *dêmos*, of the people. He is the populist, the seducer of the masses. He flatters them, he gives them what they want, or perhaps more accurately, he gives them what they think they want. As a result, they rally to his side.

What we will find in this lecture is the evolution of the demagogue into the tyrant. This is one of those instances in Book VIII and IX of the *Republic* where we find Plato being very politically astute, because the pattern he will describe is one that has been reenacted more than once in the 20th century. If we think of the great tyrants of the 20th century, many of them began precisely as Socrates says the tyrant begins, as a populist, as a benefactor to the people. Think of Hitler emerging in Germany in the '30s when people were impoverished. When the people were desperate for new direction, they rallied to his side. Think of Mussolini, who famously got the trains running on time. In other words, he improved the lives of ordinary citizens. Think of Stalin, who emerged from the Russian revolution, a revolution that claimed to be championing the poor, the disenfranchised. These revolutionaries were taken to be benefactors of the people. In this sense, they were all demagogues.

The possibility of this sort of demagoguery was far greater in Athens than it would be, or has been, in our own democratic system. This is because the democracy in Athens was, by and large, a direct democracy. In the assembly, the citizens of Athens gathered, and they would vote on just about anything. No issue would be decided outside of the assembly. Our own system—and much of it, in fact, I think was inspired by a fear of the emergence of a demagogue—our own system is not a direct democracy. Of course we have a representative democracy, and we have several, important, non-democratic features built into our own democratic system, not least of which is the Electoral College. A president isn't elected by the people, not technically. A president is elected by the Electoral College. The Supreme Court, each of the justices serves a term that lasts for his whole life, they're not subject to the whims of the people. These are just a couple of obvious features that are designed to lessen the impact of democracy in the workings of government.

The Athenians didn't have this, and, once again, this made them more subject to the kind of demagogic explosion that Socrates describes.

Let's look at the genesis of the tyrant. Of course, he poses initially as the champion of the people, especially the poor. You might look at lines 565a–c for Socrates' description of this. The next move he makes is a crucial one. He demands his own bodyguards, his own, even, private militia or army. He has an excuse; he says to the people, I am the champion of the poor, the rich hate me, the rich hate you, and I need protection from the rich. The next move he makes is a logical extension of that move, and here I'm referring to 566c. He gets a taste of blood. He does this by executing one of his enemies. He can easily explain this to his supporters; he'll say to them, he was a supporter of the rich; he was a representative of exactly that system that oppressed you so greatly. I'm your champion, excuse me for killing this person, it was in your interest for me to do this. Socrates uses a metaphor here, he says the tyrant is a cannibal who tastes blood and then wants more. In other words, as the cliché famously has it, power corrupts. Once the demagogue has committed these acts of violence against his enemies, he feels a great sense of impunity, he has the people behind him, and he becomes a full-blown tyrant. At the initial stages of his rule, he is continuing his work on behalf of the poor. Socrates says at 566e, that he releases the poor from their debts and he actually distributes land to people who were otherwise landless.

The next move he makes is to start a war with an enemy, a foreign enemy. Socrates mentions this also at 566e. The reasoning here, I think is quite predictable; when a country is attacked by a foreign enemy, the people rally around the flag. The people are in need of leadership. This is exactly what the tyrant wants. So the tyrant, and this is a hateful thing he is doing, is eager to start war, because war helps to solidify his own rule.

He continues the process of executing his enemies and he, in fact, extends this process to executing his former allies. The reason he does this is again, I think, rather predictable. The tyrant is becoming obsessed with power and the maintenance of his own power. Those people who were formally his allies are people who are potentially strong once again. No doubt, the tyrant had friends who were like him. What do we know about the tyrant? He is aggressive, he is power-hungry, he is passionate for political power, he is ruthless, and he is dangerous. So therefore, he reasons, must be these so-called friends of mine, these so-called allies. He begins the systematic process of wiping out anybody who could be a threat to him, including, perhaps especially, his former allies.

As a result of this, the tyrant is friendless. Not only is he friendless, he can't trust anybody, after all, anybody represents a potential threat. The tyrant has systematically emptied the city of all those people in it who could possibly be capable, who could be, for example, excellent military people. What the tyrant really wants is to be surrounded by flatterers, by sycophants, people who only praise him and agree with him and flatter him. This is an impoverishment of the city. Anybody worth his salt has been executed.

The tyrant begins to spend lavishly, not only to protect himself, but also to magnify his own power in the city. He might, for example, build lots of palaces. The money that should be used for the maintenance of the city is starting to flow into the tyrant's pockets. As a result of this, the rest of the city is becoming impoverished. Finally, to demonstrate the utter depravity of the tyrant, at 569b Socrates says, the tyrant is willing to kill his own father to stay in power.

One way of summarizing this whole critique of tyranny—and you can see that it, of course, is exactly that; highly, highly critical—is to say that the tyrant is a slave to his passions. He has a passionate desire for power; he is a slave to that passion because it's obliterated any sense of decency, any sense of other human beings' needs or desires. He has lost sight of the well-being of the community and only can see himself. The tyrant is a narcissist; you perhaps remember the famous myth of Narcissus. He was so impressed with his own beauty that he stared at his reflection in a pool of water and was unable to tear himself away from a vision of himself and, therefore, perished. This is the character sketch that Socrates is offering us of the tyrant.

The tyrant is "willing to act on all those savage impulses," and that's a quote from 572b, that most human beings actually have at one time or another. For example, in our dreams, we frequently dream about doing very terrible things, but the vast majority of the human race, thankfully, are able to control themselves and we don't act on these impulses. The tyrant is a slave to those impulses; he has no way of moderating himself, of correcting his behavior. He is, to summarize, friendless. He is always at risk of assassination. He is, says Socrates, unable to travel freely. He's living in an impoverished regime that's been denuded of its very best citizens.

I suggest we now take a step away from the *Republic* and look at some contemporary events, in order to see how penetrating and accurate Socrates' dissection and analysis of the tyrant really is. What I would suggest we do for a few minutes is look at the most infamous tyrant in our time, Saddam Hussein of Iraq. When you read the *Republic*, you sometimes think that Socrates is offering an analysis of someone just like Saddam Hussein, it's that accurate. Let me just remind you of a few facts about his awful career.

He joined the Baath Socialist party in 1956. It's very telling that that was a socialist party. Its claim to fame was that it was a party that was going to champion the people, distribute the wealth, precisely as Socrates says. The Baath began as the champion of the poor. By 1979, Saddam Hussein was the president of Iraq. What was the very first thing he did? He initiated an eight-year war with neighboring Iran. This war lasted from 1979–1988. Again, this conforms precisely to Socrates' diagnosis of the tyrant. The tyrant needs war with external enemies. Saddam Hussein could say to his people, these Iranians are attacking us, they hate us, and they'll destroy us; let's rally around the flag, and support me. The war was in his interest; it was his mechanism for consolidation of power. This is, to say the least, as I said before, a disgusting feature of a tyrant.

It's been said that, and I'm quoting now from the BBC News, that "Saddam is a dictator who is ready to sacrifice his country, just so long as he can remain on his throne in Baghdad." I quote that because it captures exactly the spirit, the personality, the narcissism of the tyrant as described by Socrates, and as actually appearing in our own time in the person of Saddam Hussein. Saddam Hussein killed his own people, he brutalized his own population, he used chemical weapons against the Kurds, his own fellow citizens, and he executed many of his own generals. This is one reason his own army was so inadequate; there were no excellent generals to run it. There were no excellent generals, because like every tyrant, Saddam Hussein was threatened by anyone who had any kind of military talent or ambition, they represent a threat. The only people he could tolerate were those who would flatter him, again, exactly as Socrates depicts the tyrant.

Saddam Hussein never traveled freely. In fact, he moved from one of his palaces to the next; he never slept in the same place two nights in a row. He was that fearful of assassination. You recall the Socratic description of the tyrant. Despite the fact that the tyrant sits on the throne and seems to wield such enormous power, the tyrant is actually a slave. This is precisely what happened to Saddam Hussein. He was unable to use the most simple example, to travel freely, to move on his own streets, because he had so completely alienated his own population. He had someone actually taste his own food before he ate it, he was that fearful of being poisoned. He led his country, the country of Iraq, into disaster. Iraq had great wealth from the production of oil. By the time Saddam Hussein was finished, it was impoverished and broken. As Socrates says, and I'm quoting from 576e, "There is no city more wretched than one under tyranny."

Let me next turn to another very surprising feature of Plato's *Republic*. In the previous lecture I suggested that Socrates' attitude towards democracy was surprisingly ambivalent. On the one hand, a great critic, but on the other hand, not quite as hostile as many people believed he was. Something similar will happen in his treatment of tyranny. What we're going to discover is that there is a surprising and, actually, rather disturbing similarity between the philosopher and the tyrant. There is a little textual point I would make in order to suggest to you that Plato is going to try to communicate something very important in his passage on this tyrant. It's a very long passage; it runs from pages 564–580, that's a total of 16 pages. What we discover, if you do just a little bit of calculation, is that the length of the passage that treats tyranny, the worst of the regimes, is almost exactly equal to the sum of those pages that had treated each of the previous three regimes: the timocracy, the oligarchy, and the democracy. That long passage, which treated those three regimes, ran from 547–563, also 16 pages. Plato is a very careful writer; I don't believe this is an accident. I believe it's a signal to the careful reader that something is going on in this treatment of tyranny that goes beyond its obvious import. Obviously, and very seriously, Socrates is criticizing tyranny. It's a terrible regime; make no mistake about it.

Nonetheless, underneath the surface of this treatment of tyranny is something else. What is it? I think the clue comes in line 573b. What we discover is that the tyrant, like the philosopher, is a highly erotic man, a man of great eros. That word whose basic meaning is sexual desire, but a word whose meaning Plato is continuing expanding. Perhaps it's better to translate it simply as love. The tyrant has a passionate love of political power; the philosopher has a passionate love of wisdom. This is a very real similarity between the two. I refer you again to 573b, you'll read the lines that love or eros, has from old, been called a tyrant. Eros itself is a tyrant. Well, if the philosopher is erotic, then in some sense, the philosopher has an affinity with the tyrant, and it's that affinity that I want to explore in the remainder of this lecture.

Let me take us all the way back to the very beginning; the all-important first scene in Book I of the *Republic*. The theme of eros, as I've mentioned several times, is introduced there. The old man, Cephalus, is a peaceful, calm, content old man, and he says, I'm very grateful that I'm no longer tyrannized by eros. In very blunt terms, he's rather relieved that he's no longer driven crazy by sexual desire. But I think Plato draws the scene this way to get the reader thinking about this theme of eros from the very beginning. There's a strong contrast, if you recall, between old, tired Cephalus and young, energetic Polemarchus. Polemarchus has the requisite energy to pursue the questions that Socrates is asking him. It's exactly that energy that's required in order to participate in this philosophical enterprise. The philosophical enterprise requires desire. One must want to know the answer to Socrates' questions. His questions are so hard, that only someone propelled by a very strong desire will even bother to try to answer them. Polemarchus is one such person; Glaucon is another.

What we're finding in that first scene, then, is this potentially uncomfortable connection between the philosopher and the tyrant. Let me put the point this way. A potential philosopher is like a potential tyrant. Here, I think we are well served by coming back to the character of Glaucon. Recall the beginning of Book II; Thrasymachus, who had praised the life of injustice, who in fact had praised the life that a tyrant would lead, has been defeated by Socrates. What does Glaucon do at the beginning of Book II? He says to Socrates, look, you beat him in the argument, and everybody thinks you won, but I'm not satisfied. I'm not satisfied because I am not yet completely convinced that Thrasymachus was wrong. I'm not convinced that the life of justice is intrinsically better than the life of injustice. That's what you need to prove to me.

So, you remember, perhaps, how Glaucon formulates this challenge. He tells a story, the story of the ring of Gyges. Gyges was the shepherd. One day he got hold of this magical ring; if he used this ring properly, then he became invisible. So what did he do when he learned how to manipulate the ring and become invisible whenever he wanted to? He committed crimes. He committed adultery with the queen, he killed the king, and he became, what? He became a tyrant. Glaucon suggests that this is, in fact, what most of us would really do if we had the ring of Gyges. We would commit unjust acts. What Glaucon is demanding from Socrates is a philosophical explanation that would explain why we shouldn't commit unjust acts if we could get away with that.

Let me put my point slightly differently. Glaucon clearly has a very great imagination. He's imaging this character of Gyges and what he would do if he had the ring if it made him invisible. This is a great tribute to Glaucon; it shows again, he's energetic, he's intellectual, he's challenging, he's demanding, he wants a lot from Socrates, but it also pinpoints exactly what is potentially dangerous about Glaucon. Such a person may not restrain himself sufficiently. Such a person, in short, is a potential tyrant.

This is not for Plato, writing in the 4th century, an abstract concern. I take you back to the 5th century. Plato witnessed people like Glaucon, the character I've mentioned before—these are historical figures—Alcibiades. Alcibiades was a historical figure, he was an associate of Socrates, and Socrates saw him as a potential philosopher; but in fact, Alcibiades, deep down, really wanted political power.

I mentioned the dialogue the *Charmides* written by Plato, featuring Socrates talking to the young man, Charmides, and an older man Critias. Charmides, in particular, another young man with great promise; smart, energetic, ambitious, and aggressive in some erotic, he wants a lot from life itself. In historical fact, Charmides became a tyrant; he was one of the tyrannies of the thirty. This is a genuine fear on Plato's part. I think this is why he crafted the *Republic* as a, mainly, discussion between Socrates and Glaucon. Socrates is trying to convert Glaucon, to turn his impulses away from the political to the philosophical. I'm saying all of this by way of trying to explain what I describe as this surprising and uncomfortable affinity that obtains between philosophy and tyranny. Both the tyrant and the philosopher have a disregard for convention, for traditional morality. We certainly saw that in Socrates when he opens the *Republic* by asking Cephalus, what's it like to be so old and be about to die? I described that as a very rude and aggressive question, and I believe it is. It's an innocuous question in terms of philosophical explanation, but Plato's genius is to locate serious issues in the small, seemingly innocuous exchanges.

You've read the *Republic*; perhaps, you've read other dialogues by Plato. One response students regularly have to Socrates is, he's a bully, he's always making people answer his questions, and he's always dictating the rules of the conversation. That's not a misleading impression. He is a kind of bully; that's another way of saying he is not entirely dissimilar to a tyrant.

Let me refer you to line 578c, this is still Socrates' discussion of the tyrant. In fact, what he does in this passage is say there really are two kinds of tyrants. There is, what we might call, private tyrants, and then there are public tyrants. A public or political tyrant is the person who actually lives out the tyrannical desires in the political skew. Now, Socrates doesn't tell us who the private tyrant would be. It's one of these mysteries in the *Republic*; it's one of these occasions where I'm quite confident, that Plato is asking the reader to think for himself or for herself. Who would be the private tyrant? Maybe it's the person who is tyrannized by the love of wisdom.

I mean, I would ask you just to reflect a little bit on what it means to really fall in love. We all know what it's like to fall in love with a person, but we also fall in love with other things. You might fall in love with opera, or you might fall in love with painting, or you might fall in love, as I have, with the Boston Red Sox. These are desires that are potentially tyrannical; they will dominate your life. You'll try to get them out of your head and you can't do it. Perhaps, the philosopher is such a person, tyrannized by the love of wisdom, and unwilling to pursue any other object except wisdom itself. I would suggest that's not a bad description of our friend Socrates.

Lecture Twenty
Book IX—The Superiority of Justice

Scope:

Socrates argues that the life of the just philosopher is happier and more pleasant than that of the unjust tyrant. With this argument, he returns, finally, to the challenge posed by Thrasymachus in Book I; namely, to show that one ought to prefer a life of justice to a life of injustice. In completing this argument, Socrates offers yet another image. This time, he sketches a strange picture of both a lion, a many-headed beast, and a human being living within each human being. We will discuss this image in detail and see how it complements the psychology Socrates offered in Book IV.

We will conclude this lecture by examining one passage: "Perhaps a pattern is laid up for the man who wants to see and found a city within himself on the basis of what he sees. It doesn't make any difference whether it is or will be somewhere" (592b).

Outline

I. Socrates addresses the challenge issued by Glaucon and Adeimantus: to demonstrate that Thrasymachus was wrong and that a life of justice is superior to a life of injustice.

    A. The main reason is that, as discussed in the previous lecture, the real tyrant is a slave to his passions (579e).

    B. Socrates explains this by returning to the tripartite psychology he developed in Book IV.

    C. There are three parts of the soul: wisdom-loving, victory-loving, gain-loving (581c). In Book IV, these were called reason, spirit, and desire.

    D. The entire soul is now characterized by "love."

    E. The life of the just man, ruled by the love of wisdom, is more pleasant than that of the unjust man.

        1. The lover of wisdom has tasted all the pleasures. The lover of gain and the lover of honor, by contrast, have never tasted the pleasure of philosophy (582a).

        2. Therefore, the lover of wisdom has the most pleasure.

3. Further, the pleasure experienced by the lover of wisdom is the most pure. It does not entail its opposite: pain (584b).

4. The object of philosophy is "being," that is, what is stable and "really real." Therefore, the pleasure associated with it is stable (584c).

5. Socrates tells a joke: The philosopher-king "lives 729 times more pleasantly" (587e) than the tyrant. (There are 729 days and nights in one year.)

6. The answer to why philosophy is superior to life's other pursuits is found in the *Republic* as a whole. It teaches us what it is to be a human being, what it is to have a soul.

F. At the end of the *Republic*, it is unclear whether Socrates is talking about justice as it is conventionally understood or the sort of harmony that was discussed in Book IV—reason ruling desire with the assistance of the spirit..

II. Socrates proposes a new image of the human soul.

A. A many-headed beast represents desire, a lion represents spirit, and a human being represents reason. All three are contained within the human soul (588c–e).

B. The image suggests the basic reason why justice should be pursued: It is most human (589a–b).

Essential Reading:

Plato's Republic, Book IX.

Supplementary Reading:

Sachs, D. "A Fallacy in Plato's *Republic*," in R. Kraut, ed., *Plato's Republic: Critical Essays*, pp. 1–17.

Questions to Consider:

1. Review Socrates's argument about pleasure. He seems to imply that some pleasures are superior to others. Is this true, or are all pleasures equal?

2. Socrates seems to state that it doesn't matter whether his ideal city comes into existence or not. If this is the case, then why do you think he bothered to construct an ideal city?

Lecture Twenty—Transcript
Book IX—The Superiority of Justice

We've reached Book IX of Plato's *Republic*. We're getting close to the finish line. Socrates has finished the entire exercise that he promised to complete. He has constructed what he claims is a perfectly just city and he has also analyzed the various forms of injustice. He is now prepared, in a final way, to address the original question posed to him by Glaucon: why prefer a life of justice to a life of injustice? Why not, if we could get away with it, lead a life in which we committed unjust acts and simply attempted to maximize our own self-interest, even if it meant trampling over the interests of others? In short, Socrates is finally prepared to answer, once and for all, the challenge proposed by Thrasymachus in Book I.

We've seen the real answer to the question already. It was contained in the analysis of the tyrant. The tyrant is the maximally unjust human being. The tyrant, you recall, was described as being a slave. He seems to be on top of the world, he seems to be the political leader of his own country, in fact he's no more than a slave; he is a slave to his passions. Socrates elaborates this argument in several ways in Book IX and that's what we will discuss in this lecture.

To do this, he returns to a subject we broached in Lecture Four. This is often referred to as Plato's "tripartite psychology." This is the psychological scheme in which the human psyche, often translated as soul, is said to have three parts: reason, spirit, and desire. Socrates returns to this tripartite scheme in Book IX, but in a very interesting way, he subtly, but significantly reformulates the three parts. Instead of being reason, spirit, and desire, we find at 581c, these three parts: there is the wisdom loving, the victory loving, and the gain loving. Clearly corresponding to reason, spirit, and desire, but significantly reformulated, because now each of the parts is said to be in love; in love with an object, whether the object is wisdom, victory, or gain.

This, I hope, substantiates one of the claims I've made a few times in our course, and that is, for Plato, the very essence of the human psyche, the human soul, is eros, is love. Because now we see that even these seemingly distinct parts of the soul are unified by the fact that each one of them is described as a form of love. In this sense, the soul is really nothing but love. What differentiates one soul from another is what it loves. The oligarch, for example, loves gain, the timocrat loves honor, and the philosopher loves wisdom.

Socrates then turns to a new issue. It's not really new, it's a new perspective on the old question, why prefer justice to injustice, and he argues that, in fact, the just person has a life that's vastly more pleasurable than anyone else. If you recall a comment I made much earlier in our course when I was describing the position of hedonism. Hedonism is that position which equates pleasure and the good. For the hedonist, if something is pleasurable, it's good, period, end of story. Socrates rejects hedonism and he rejects it by means of the following argument. He insists that there are good pleasures and bad pleasures. Once that distinction is made, as we've discussed, there is a standard higher than pleasure that's invoked in order to measure pleasures. So pleasure is not the good, good pleasure is good. What Socrates is arguing in this section of the *Republic* is that justice—in fact, philosophy, because we know that the just ruler is the philosopher—gives us the highest and best form of pleasure.

So what I would like to do next is review three of the arguments that Socrates gives on behalf of this thesis. I warn you in advance that you may not be entirely satisfied by these arguments. If that were the case, I would urge you to be patient with Plato, because in fact, I suspect that these arguments are not satisfying and that Plato understands that they're not satisfying. He has something else in mind, as he usually does. He has a little trick up his sleeve.

The first argument is the argument on behalf of the idea that philosophy actually gives us the best of pleasure. The argument here is that the philosopher is the best judge of pleasure. The philosopher is the best critic. Why is that? It's because the philosopher has tasted every kind of pleasure. The philosopher knows what it is to feel pleasure from gain. The philosopher knows what it is to feel pleasure from honor. The competitors, however, have not tasted the pleasure of wisdom, and therefore, they are in an inferior position to make a judgment about what is the best pleasure. It follows, again, that if the philosopher is the best judge, then the pleasure that the philosopher chooses, must be the best pleasure. And of course we know what pleasure that would be, it's the pleasure of philosophy. Socrates believes he's won his point. I would urge you on your own to review the steps of this argument, and you try to figure out for yourself if you think it holds water. As I suggested, it may very well not.

Second argument: the pleasure that arises from the love of wisdom, unlike other pleasures, does not give rise to its opposite, pain. It is a pure pleasure. The argument for this position is given at 584b. What does Socrates have in mind? Well, the easiest contrast to make is the hangover. We have a wonderful night of eating and drinking and drinking and drinking, a lot of pleasure, yes, but we pay a big price the next day. Socrates suggests that, in fact, all physical pleasures are like this. Even if they're not as overtly connected to pain as the hangover, they are, nonetheless, caught up in this same transitioning from pleasure to pain, from pain to pleasure. Philosophy, by contrast, he argues, is a pure pleasure. There is no pain that follows the pleasures that we gain from the study of philosophy. Again, perhaps it is not the most satisfying argument, but certainly interesting.

The third argument is very much related to the second, and this I'm referring to, is found at 584c. The object of philosophy, the goal of philosophical inquiry, is "being." That's a term we've used several times, especially in conjunction with the famous platonic forms and the Idea of the Good. The salient feature of being is that it's permanent; it's stable, changeless, eternal, and perfect in every way. The key word here is stable. If the philosopher aims to articulate and understand being itself; if the philosopher aims, for example, to move up the Divided-Line—start at the bottom in the realm of images, and move all the way up to the top, the Idea of the Good— such a person, say Socrates here in Book IX, is going to engage in a kind of pleasure that's very stable. The pleasure one feels from studying being, Socrates says, is as stable as the object itself, namely, being.

This may not be very clear, so let me illustrate it again by means of a contrast. Let's go back to our old friend, the oligarch. The oligarch loves profit, gain, and money. What do we know about people who love money? I'll speak anachronistically here. Someone who loves money might invest very heavily in the stock market and the stock market goes way up, and such a person is very happy, feels a lot of pleasure, but anybody who has invested in the market knows that what goes up, must come down. So, the person who's made a killing in the stock market and feels pleasure doesn't find that pleasure lasting very long. Either the stock market will crash and then this person will feel a lot of pain, or even if it doesn't crash, this person will feel what? This person will feel anxiety, stress. If you have money, you worry about money. Money, in this case, is an example of a very unstable object. The stock market is the best example of that. Being, by the contrast, doesn't go up and down; there are no fluctuations in being. Being is not subject to market forces. Therefore, the pleasure gained by the study of being, is a very enduring, stable pleasure. Another way to put this is no one can take being away. If I'm a student of being, I don't have to fear that somebody's going to steal it from me. If I have a lot of money, I might very well worry that somebody will steal it from me. If I'm engaged in pleasures of the body, I might very well worry that when I get old, I won't be able to experience these pleasures. If I'm a lover of the body, I will probably, above all else, fear death, because death would mean the termination of my pleasures. Again, by contrast, the lover of philosophy, the lover of being, has no such anxiety to plague him.

The more you read Plato's dialogues, not just the *Republic*, the more you'll feel this sense of pleasure in the character. Socrates never seems to get upset. He's famous for only laughing three times, and we never see him cry. He doesn't seem to experience any of the stress, anxiety, that we and, of course, ancient Athenians were so familiar with. He seems to lead a life of constant, stable pleasure. Again, when I speak of Socrates, I refer only to the character appearing in Plato's dialogue. Did the real Socrates live this way? Who knows; we can't know. But as a character created by Plato, inspired by a historical figure, but no doubt filled with Plato's imagination, the character clearly is meant to express just this idea. That a lover of wisdom doesn't suffer the ups and downs, the hangovers, and the stresses, that the lover of gain or the lover of honor will regularly experience.

One last word about the lover of honor; it's a very important point. We might think of the lover of honor also as a lover of fame, loves recognition. Well, such a person might get great pleasure from fame and recognition, but the public is very fickle. So, therefore, such a person will, once again, be in a state of stress, and therefore, the pleasure gained by fame is fleeting and unstable. The contrast with philosophy can be made again.

These arguments about pleasure are designed to remind us of the essential task Socrates believes he has now completed: to demonstrate to Glaucon that the life of philosophy is in every which way superior to any other life. In particularly, it's most superior to the life of the tyrant, the person who is able, apparently, to maximize his own self-interest.

At this point, and the point I'm referring to in the text is found at 587e, Socrates makes a joke. Not a joke that will cause you to laugh out loud, but a subtle philosophical joke. Socrates says the philosopher—the philosopher king, the philosopher ruler, the philosopher queen, the thoroughly just philosophical soul that we've explored for all these many pages—lives 729 times more pleasantly than the tyrant. So, the best life is precisely 729 times better than the worst one. This is a joke because who could possibly demonstrate with such mathematical precision that one life is 729 times better, more pleasant, than another life. The joke seems to be based, as Socrates later mentions, on the notion that in a year, a calendar year, there are 729 days and nights total. So, it seems to be an indication of the complete superiority of the philosophical life.

Let me suggest something else about this joke. It opens up a theme we've explored more than once in this course. That's the relationship between mathematics and the human soul. It is manifestly absurd to think you could calculate the superiority of a life and come up with a number as precise as 729. But what's the point of the joke? The point of the joke is similar to a point I made about the marriage number in Book XIII of the *Republic*. If you recall that passage, it's near the beginning of Book VIII, the perfectly just city must regulate sexual reproduction. It must develop, what today we would call, the science of genetic engineering or eugenics. The marriage number is a very obscure passage; we can't fathom the mathematics there, but the point is clear. The rulers fail to calculate the marriage number. In other words, they fail to arrive at a mathematically based science, which would be able to control eros. At the beginning of this lecture I suggested that eros is shorthand for the human soul, the human psyche. The marriage number, therefore, represents the failure of mathematics to capture what is most human.

We know very well that Plato was a lover of mathematics, but he did not take mathematics and place it at the absolute pinnacle of intellectual endeavors. Mathematics is good, but it's not that good. It's not as good as philosophy, and philosophy is not equivalent to mathematics. What is philosophy? Philosophy is what we find in Plato's *Republic*; it's conversation, it is dialectic. It is human beings talking to each other, using old-fashioned regular language, not mathematics. So, unlike many modern thinkers, Plato relegates mathematics to a subordinate role. Good, but not the best.

I think the joke that's found at 587e in Book IX is a similar reminder of this point. It would also explain an earlier suggestion I made. The various arguments that Socrates gave us concerning the superiority of philosophical pleasure were not entirely convincing. They were not convincing, not because Socrates doesn't believe his conclusion. He does think that philosophy is the best and most pleasurable form of life, but I don't think he believes that there is a single argument, some sort of logical train of thought that, in a nutshell, could prove the way a mathematical equation might prove its result. The true argument for why philosophy is superior to any other form of life, particularly that of the tyrant, is given in the *Republic* as a whole. Not restricted to just these little three arguments we reviewed earlier, it's the entire *Republic* in which we gain an understanding of what it means to be a human being. I believe that is the ultimate teaching of the *Republic*; it's teaching us what it is to have a soul.

At this point, let me mention a very famous problem that scholars have identified in the *Republic*. An author named David Sachs— you'll find his article in your bibliographies—made this point in an article that has been much discussed. At the end of the *Republic*, it's unclear whether Socrates is talking about justice in a normal way, or whether he is talking about philosophical justice in the extraordinary sense that he has developed his own ideas through the course of the *Republic*. The title of David Sachs's article is "A Fallacy of Irrelevance in Plato's *Republic*." What he means by irrelevance is, at the very beginning of the *Republic*, the encounter with Thrasymachus and then with Glaucon that we've discussed at such length, the challenge is to demonstrate that a life of justice is superior to a life of injustice. Now, what Thrasymachus has in mind when he defends the life of injustice is, you might say, ordinary, run-of-the-mill injustice, robbing people, being unfair, taking advantage of a political system rather than being concerned with the well-being of the whole. It therefore seems that what Socrates is required to do in order to respond adequately to Thrasymachus, is defend the life of, let's call it, run-of-the-mill justice; obeying the law, not robbing people, caring about the community in ways that we would all associate with justice, as it is conventionally understood.

Of course, as you now know from studying Plato's *Republic*, the justice that Socrates actually discusses throughout the long, long process that is this dialogue, goes far beyond the run-of-the-mill, the ordinary. It seems that what he's discussing, and this has been apparent in the way I've developed my own terminology in this course, is philosophical justice. Justice, at the end of Book IV, is the "harmony of the soul." Reason ruling desire with the assistance of spirit; justice is philosophical harmony of the soul. It's the love of wisdom. Now, I think what some critics might say is, Socrates, you did a really great job explaining that to us, but you never really explained run-of-the-mill justice, why is that superior? "I believe you," I can imagine the critics saying, "that philosophy is superior to injustice, but why is conventional justice superior to justice?"

What this suggests is that the real concern of Plato's *Republic* is philosophy itself. It's actually not justice, at least not justice in the ordinary sense of the term. We have been moving, as you are surely aware, further and further away from the ordinary concerns of an ordinary city. We've been moving, to use the language of the parable of the cave, closer and closer to the sun, leaving the cave behind. I think that's a very deliberate thrust of the *Republic*. Plato crafts his dialogue precisely to make that point, that the truest concern for justice leads actually away from the city, towards philosophy; we'll come back to that point.

Let me close this section with a brief look at another extraordinary passage in Book IX; it occurs at 588c–e. Here, what Socrates does is, once again, reformulate his tripartite psychology. We've had reason, spirit, and desire; we've had the wisdom lover, the gain lover, and the honor lover; and now, what Socrates does is construct an image. A picture, which is meant to capture this sense of the tripartite psychology, but, as we'll see, it also changes it in a very significant way.

What we should do is the following, says Socrates. Let's draw a picture in which a many-headed beast known as the Hydra represents desire. We'll have a lion, and we'll use a human being to represent reason, the three parts. We will then enclose all three parts in a human being. This is now the picture of the human soul. This image, once again, is used in order to make the basic point that Socrates wishes to make, and that is that a life of justice should be pursued. Justice is when reason rules the soul. We now know that reason is the most human of those three beasts inside of a human being, and so therefore, another way to put Socrates' point is that justice is more human than injustice. The person who would get away with doing injustice becomes more like a beast than a human being.

This is a very odd picture, and you can figure out why if you either draw it or just try to imagine it. Recall, inside a human being is a Hydra, the many-headed beast, a lion, and a human being. It's that last item that makes it so peculiar, because if there is a human being inside of a human being, then presumably within that human being is a Hydra, a lion, and a human being. And inside that human being, the same three appear. What this suggests is we are on an infinite loop, which is an impossible picture. This is the way some commentators describe this last picture. It's actually a non-picture. It is not a formal structure. It can't be, because it infinitely expands.

Now, I believe this is entirely deliberate on Plato's part to have Socrates offer this revision of the tripartite psychology, and it goes back to the same theme I've been making for much of this lecture. I mentioned the failure of the marriage number and the joke about the life of philosophy being so precisely superior to the life of injustice, that we can calculate it at 729. The importance of those passages was to suggest that mathematics couldn't capture the human soul. I think the picture at 588c—or rather the non-picture—makes the same point. Compare it to the tripartite psychology of Book IV, three separate parts; reason, spirit, and desire. They are static, they are rigidly structured, and, as we discussed when we were discussing Book IV, it's an incoherent scheme. What made that scheme in Book IV incoherent is that it required reason to give orders to desire, but desire is so separated from reason, that it would be unable to comprehend the orders.

In sum, the tripartite scheme of Book IV is too mathematical, it's too rigid, and each of those three parts is like a separate unit, like a number. Whereas the last image that we find in Book IX, I would suggest, is much more authentically human, precisely because it's not so rigid. It's in constant motion; it's in a mode of expansion. That is much more of an accurate sense of what the human soul really is.

Lecture Twenty-One
Book X—Philosophy versus Poetry

Scope:

Despite the fact that he discussed poetry at length in Books II and III, Socrates returns to this topic in Book X. This time, his critique is even more severe. While a certain kind of poetry was allowed in Book III—what Socrates calls the "unmixed imitation of the decent" (397d—in Book X, all poetic imitation is condemned. Socrates offers two arguments to bolster his extreme position. The first is metaphysical; the second is psychological. We will discuss both in detail. We will conclude with some general reflections on what Socrates calls the "old quarrel between philosophy and poetry" (607b). We will try to understand why he thinks that these two most basic forms of human intellectual activity are at odds with each other.

Outline

I. In Book IX, Socrates reiterates that his just city is not a blueprint for political action.

   A. He says the job of the philosopher is to look within himself (591e).

   B. There, he will find a pattern of a just city. It doesn't matter whether this city actually comes into being (592b).

   C. The *Republic* is about the human soul; it is intended to teach us something about ourselves.

II. In Books II and III, Socrates recommended censoring poetry. In Book X, he offers an even more forceful denunciation of it.

   A. Socrates applies the term *poetry* to all forms of storytelling.

   B. His first argument is a "metaphysical critique" of poetry.

   1. There is "one particular 'form' for each of the particular 'manys' to which we apply the same name" (596a).

   2. This is a version of the theory of Ideas.

   3. For example, there is one "idea of the couch" and many particular couches.

   4. God produced the idea of the couch (597b).

5. A carpenter builds a couch.

6. A painter imitates the carpenter's couch in his painting.

7. Therefore, imitation takes us far from the truth. It is two steps removed from reality. (See 599a.)

C. The second argument is a psychological critique of poetry.

   1. Because poetry depends on images and tells emotionally charged stories, it nourishes the irrational part of the human soul. (See 603b.)

   2. Poetry, particularly tragedy, imitates men who are conflicted (604a). This is what makes a play "dramatic."

   3. But the good man, whose soul is harmonious, experiences no such conflict.

   4. Therefore, poetry encourages psychological discord.

   5. The characters in a play experience a wild array of emotions. The good man is self-controlled and "quiet."

   6. The comic poet makes us laugh at things (such as sexual activities) that we would otherwise be too ashamed to laugh at (606c).

D. "There is an old quarrel between philosophy and poetry" (607b), which Socrates resolves, essentially, by banning the poets.

III. The critique of poetry in Book X is even more severe than the censorship program of Books II and III. Why?

A. Poetry is a fundamental alternative to philosophy.

B. Yet Socrates says that if a poet could make an argument to defend his poetry, then "we should be delighted to receive it" (607c).

   1. A philosophical form of poetry seems acceptable.

   2. Perhaps the Platonic dialogues themselves are such a form of poetry.

   3. The *Republic* itself violates the rules against poetry!

C. Socrates draws a comparison between Sophistry, which uses persuasive rhetoric, and poetry. Both make their own truths. Even Socrates himself borrows the rhetorical techniques of the Sophists and the storytelling art of poets to make his points. He respects the power of poetry and Sophistry.

Essential Reading:

Plato's Republic, Book X.

Supplementary Reading:

Roochnik, D. *Beautiful City: The Dialectical Character of Plato's Republic*, pp. 93–125.

Urmson, James. "Plato and the Poets," in R. Kraut, ed., *Plato's Republic: Critical Essays*, pp. 223–234.

Questions to Consider:

1. Do you think there are ideas, or "truths," that a poem (or a story) can express that an argument cannot? Why or why not?

2. Why do you think Plato wrote dialogues instead of abstract arguments?

Lecture Twenty-One—Transcript
Book X—Philosophy versus Poetry

In this lecture we're going to concentrate on Book X, the very last book of Plato's *Republic*. Before we do so, however, I'd like to take one last look at the very end of Book IX, because Socrates makes a couple of remarks there that I think are worth paying attention to, and I'm referring now to lines 591e–592b.

What Socrates says there is that the job of the philosopher is to look within, to look within and see a regime, a political regime within himself. He then says that having looked within, what the philosopher will see is a pattern of a well organized, just city. Once again, this is within the soul of the philosopher. And then, most strikingly, he says, it doesn't matter if this city that the philosopher glimpses ever actually comes into being.

I think these lines are important, because they remind us of a theme I've been developing in the last several lectures. The ultimate purpose of Plato's *Republic* may not be to actually create a blueprint for a city that could actually come into existence. Instead, what I believe the *Republic* is finally aiming at is precisely what Socrates has just noted at the end of Book IX, an "internal city," if I can put it in those terms.

The *Republic* is finally about the human soul; it's not a book that is devoted to the construction or even to the hope of constructing a real city on earth. I make this point with some emphasis because I'm certain that some of you in learning about Plato's *Republic* feel a sense of, perhaps, even revulsion. After all, the regime he constructs in the earlier books seems totalitarian—the family is obliterated, private property is obliterated, and all interests are subordinated to the city. I'm suggesting a way of softening your reaction to the *Republic*, and I'm taking my bearings from the last remarks that Socrates himself makes; suggesting, implicitly and nearly explicitly, that the real goal of the *Republic* is to teach us something about ourselves and not to start a political program that we hope to put into actual practice.

Now we can turn to Book X. This is a very surprising book. This is a book which has given scholars fits for centuries, because we learn, upon opening Book X, that Socrates takes up an issue that we readers would have suspected is long finished, and the issue is poetry. You recall that a huge portion of Books II and III were devoted to the censorship program, mainly focusing on the censorship of literature. Homer, Hesiod, the Tragedians, and the comic playwrights, they're all severely regulated in the city Socrates constructs. Having completed that, we might wonder, why in the world does Socrates return to the issue of poetry at the beginning of Book X?

Let me make one point before I go any further. I want to explain this word poetry. When we use it in English we are referring to a rather narrow genre of literature. The word poetry, as Plato would use it, is much wider in its meaning. It's interesting to look at the etymology of our own word poetry. It comes from the Greek word *poësis*, which means, "to make." Poetry, as a Greek would use the word, refers almost to all kinds of artistic production, artistic making, in general. It certainly is not restricted to what we, in English, would call poetry. It refers, most importantly, to all forms of storytelling. When you tell a story, what do you do? You make it up. That little English phrase is very telling, and goes right to the heart of what the word poetry means for Plato.

Again, Socrates, as he so often does, surprises us in Book X, because not only does he revisit the issue of poetry, but he now also offers an even more severe criticism of it. If in Books II and III he censored the poets, if he regulated and restricted their creativity, in Book X he comes very close to banishing the poets all together. This has become a notorious passage in the history of western culture. It's often pointed to as the best evidence of Plato's hatred of art. We'll investigate that claim in this lecture.

Socrates gives two arguments against poetry. The first is usually called by scholars, the metaphysical critique of poetry. In order to make this criticism, Socrates first reviews some of the basic elements of his famous theory of Forms. I would refer you here to 596a. Socrates says the following, There is "one particular 'form' for each of the particular 'manys' to which we apply the same name" That's a very useful line to review, because it very nicely summarizes much of what we discussed about the theory of Forms earlier in this course. Notice the last couple of words, "the same name." Remember, as I suggested to you earlier; the theory of Forms really takes its bearings, one might almost say, gets its inspiration, from language. We have a single word, say the word chair. That single word has a very general meaning, and it refers to all the many particular chairs that exist in the world. Every single one of them is different from each other, but they're all united by being a chair. There is a one, the one chair, and then there are the many chairs. That one chair is what Socrates calls the idea of the chair or the form of the chair. Remember those two words, idea and form, are synonyms.

The next move Socrates makes is even more shocking than the fact that he is revisiting the theme of poetry. He says there is a God and God produced the ideas. He uses as his example, the idea of the couch, a very ordinary, lowly object, I'm referring here to 597b. Now, this truly has given scholars fits, because it doesn't seem to cohere with so much else that we've heard Plato say about his theory of Ideas. Nowhere else in the *Republic* has he mentioned some sort of creative God who is able to make the ideas, make the forms. In fact, that notion of a creative God actually contradicts some of the things he says about the forms in Book VI and Book VII, because one important feature of the forms is that they are permanent or eternal. They do not come into being. However, if here in Book X we're told that God makes the ideas, then they do come into being and they're not eternal. This is a problem—a real problem—and I'll try to address it, give you some suggestion about how to think about it, at the very end of this lecture.

So first step, God makes the idea of the couch; second step, a carpenter, who imitates the idea of the couch, builds a couch using wood. He builds a particular couch. Third step, a painter imitates the couch that the carpenter built and draws a painting. The key word in this discussion is "imitation." Again, a very broad word, it means any form of artistic representation. From this metaphysical scheme—and the word metaphysical comes very close to a word we've discussed, the word ontological—metaphysics is a conception of reality. So, a metaphysical scheme is a scheme about reality. From this metaphysical scheme, God makes the idea of the couch, carpenter builds the couch, and painter imitates the carpenter's couch. Socrates concludes, and now I'm referring to 598b, that imitation is very far from the truth. It's two big steps removed from the truth. The truth is found, of course, in the forms, in the ideas. The painter doesn't even have access to them; the painter's access to the form is mediated by the carpenter's couch, that's what the painter paints.

Socrates expresses this by saying at 599a, that imitation, in general, again, artistic representation, is third from what is; third from being. Therefore, it's intrinsically deficient. This is the metaphysical critique of poetry, poetry understood in its very broad sense, to embrace close to all forms of artistic making.

Second argument that Socrates offers against poetry, and this one is more focused on poetry a bit more narrowly construed as literature, is a psychological critique. Let's use drama as our example; I believe it is what Socrates has in mind here. When you go to the theater—and the Greeks love the theater—we find on stage, imitations of real people. They're in costume, they're play-acting, they are in the Greek theater, wearing masks, and we get involved in the events that take place on stage. These are not real events; these, of course, are artistic representations. These artistic representations require images and these artistic representations generate tremendous, emotional reaction in the audience. This is, of course, the heart and soul of drama.

When we go to the theater, for example, we might see Sophocles's great play, *Oedipus* the *King*. We see a very good man, Oedipus, suffering terribly. He has inadvertently killed his father and his mother. Through no real fault of his own, he suffers an extraordinary fate. The audience feels pity, the audience feels fear, and the audience is caught up in this grand imitation, in these beautiful words, in the images that are on stage. All of this, which might sound pretty good to some people, is exactly what Socrates, here, is criticizing about poetry. The way he puts it is that poetry—and again let's use drama as our example—nourishes the irrational part of the soul. What's that irrational part of the soul? Our desires, our emotions; it's not our reason.

If we didn't have emotional reactions in the theater, the play we were watching, we would say, is not a good play. Remember Socrates's model of a just human being, especially in Book IV. You recall that the soul is always described as having three parts: reason, spirit, and desire. Spirit is very much an emotion; and the just human being, says Socrates, is harmonious. Reason controls desire, spirit is the ally of reason in the control of desire. Such a human being, a good human being according to Socrates's argument, would be very calm, very rational, very collected. Exactly not like the person we see on stage. The very essence, I think, of drama is conflict. If there were no conflict that the character faced, the play simply wouldn't be interesting. But it's exactly conflict that Socrates has been trying to eliminate for the entirety of the *Republic*.

First and foremost in his constructed city, he was trying to eliminate conflict between citizens. And then when we made the transfer into the individual soul, he is trying to eliminate internal conflict. Unlike a person who is at war with himself because he can't control his own desires, the Socratic model is one of the absences of conflict, of harmony. This is, yet again, the opposite of what we see in Greek tragedy, and that's why Socrates here in Book X suggests, let's get rid of it. It's bad, it nourishes, it supports, and it reinforces what's not the best part of us; what is, in fact, the lowest part of us.

This same sort of critique would apply, and Socrates makes this point explicit at 606c, to comedy. Comedy in the 5th century, in the 4th century, in ancient Greece was not so different from our own versions of comedy. In any comedy that we would watch today or an ancient Greek would watch, there'd be plenty of dirty jokes, jokes about the body. The body tends to be a very funny subject when it's displayed on stage. What happens when we go to the theater to watch a comedy, says Socrates, is that we laugh at things we would be ashamed of laughing at if we were at home alone. We laugh at things we would never even make public in private. So comedy, Socrates is arguing here in Book X, brings out the worst in us. And therefore, he concludes, 605b, we should not admit, not allow, poets into our city—a very, very radical condemnation of poetry.

The phrase Socrates uses to summarize this line of thought is found at 607b. He describes "an old quarrel between philosophy and poetry." The two are at war with each other, and we have had some suggestions as to why this is the case. The philosopher—and of course it's the philosopher who rules in Socrates's constructed city—the philosopher is the supremely rational human being whose desires are at service of reason. The philosopher is a soul utterly dominated by reason. Going to the theater, whether it's a tragedy or a comedy, threatens to disrupt that nice pattern of harmony.

Let me now offer you some speculations and, here, as I've tried to do throughout this course, I must identify these as my interpretations. This is a very mysterious chapter in Plato's *Republic*, Book X, for the reasons I've already mentioned to you, and a commentator must do some speculating; there's no way out. So, I will offer you some suggestions and ask you to think about them critically and perhaps even try to come up with your own.

Here's the first question. Why is this critique of poetry found in Book X, so much more severe than the censorship found in Books II and III? Censorship is bad enough, but at least it allows some form of poetry to exist in the city. In Book X, there is none. Well, let me suggest an idea that comes very close to being paradoxical. I think Socrates is so critical of poetry in Book X, because he respects it so much. You might think of a relationship anyone of us has to an opponent. Think, for example, if you're an athlete. If you're an athlete, you develop a very complicated relationship to your opponent, especially if you have an opponent who really challenges you. If you're a tennis player and you're much, much better than your opponent, you can defeat her easily; that's not a very interesting game. If, by contrast, your opponent is as good as you are or perhaps even a little better, it's a terrific match. Maybe you win, maybe you lose, but at the end of the day, you know you've been pushed so hard by your opponent that as a result, you have a respect, an affection even, for your opponent, even though you just spent such a grueling couple of hours trying to defeat her. I would suggest that something like this is going on in Socrates's relationship to poetry. It is his opponent, he is critical of it, but at the same time, he acknowledges its immense power, its immense role that it plays in human culture.

Another way to put this point is that he acknowledges that poetry is a fundamental human option. It's a fundamental alternative to philosophy and it can't simply be refuted. It won't disappear; no one is going to read the arguments in Book X of the *Republic* and then say, okay, I'll never write any more poetry; I won't go to any more plays. That sort of artistic production has such a pull on us; we'll never let it go. I think Plato understands this very well.

Now let me suggest you read 607c with some care, because it's another one of these rather surprising lines that we so often find in the *Republic*. He says that if there could be an argument that a poet could make to defend his poetry, then, in fact, we would be delighted to receive it into the city. I would describe that line as a door opener; it opens the door to the possibility of what I would describe as a philosophical form of poetry. If a kind of poetry could emerge which would explain itself, justify itself, articulate itself philosophically, then it would be acceptable in the very city that just a few lines earlier had banished the poets.

Let me make a radical suggestion, one that you should take with a grain of salt. I would suggest that the platonic dialogues themselves, the *Republic* in particular, are exactly this, a philosophical form of poetry. Let's just take a step back and think about the *Republic* in rather common-sensical terms. What do we discover? Well, we discover, first of all, it's a lot like a drama. There are plenty of characters, and the author of this drama, Plato, imitates them. When you're reading Book I, you meet this old man, Cephalus, and then you meet this younger man, Polemarchus, and then we meet this extremely hot headed man, Thrasymachus. These are all very lifelike characters, and you, as a reader, are caught up in the drama of Socrates trying to refute them.

Well, this is very peculiar, because what we're discovering is that Plato himself violates his own strictures against poetry in the *Republic* itself. I think he's playing a little trick on us, us the readers. He's criticizing poetry, but he's actually writing a poem. Again, remember poem is a much broader word than we typically take it to be. He's writing a poem in which one of the characters, Socrates, criticizes poetry.

Let me give another example of how Plato plays this trick on us, and here I'll go back a little bit to Book II. If you recall, the story lines of all literature are severely censored in Book II and in Book III, and one of the prohibitions that Socrates insists upon is that we're not going to have stories in which just men are unhappy and unjust men are happy. That's a very dangerous story because we would use it to discourage people from being just. If we tell stories in which just people come to bad endings, then we might have a deleterious effect on our citizens; that was the rationale in Book II. But let's never forget the story—and that is what it is—that actually sparks the entire *Republic*, and that's the story Glaucon tells about the ring of Gyges. And here we have a man who steals a ring, uses it to become invisible, sleeps with the queen, kills the king, he is not a just man, and he seems to flourish. Now, that's a story that Glaucon tells in order to provoke Socrates to refute it. Nonetheless, Glaucon tells a story that would itself be prohibited in the city that Socrates constructs, another example of the sort of trick I think Plato is playing on us. He is trying to show us implicitly that while, yes, poetry is to be criticized, at the same time, it's not actually to be completely banished, and it's actually present in the *Republic* itself.

In this regard, let me make a comparison between Socrates's attitude towards poetry and his attitude towards Sophistry. Remember, Thrasymachus is a Sophist, he is a relativist, and he practices the art of rhetoric. In many dialogues Socrates draws a comparison between the Sophist and the poet. Recall that the relativist denies that there is any absolute truth and, instead, insists that all truth, all values, are relative to a particular context or social group. In this country, freedom of speech is counted to be a good thing; in that country, it's counted to be a bad thing. Freedom of speech is neither good nor bad; it depends who holds the view.

Rhetoric plays such an important role in the relativist world of the Sophist, because it's by means of rhetoric that any given value, any given truth, comes into being. If I can manage to persuade the citizens of my city to believe that freedom of speech is a good thing, then freedom of speech will be counted as a good thing. It's not absolutely good, it's not objectively good, and it's good in my city. Why is it good? It's good because I made it good. I constructed a view, and I persuaded other people to buy into my view. I use the word make deliberately to draw the connection between Sophistry and poetry. Both of them imply that human beings don't see the truth, they make the truth, or more accurately, they make lots and lots and lots of truths.

I would suggest that Plato has a very similar attitude to Sophistry and to poetry. He's very critical of both, neither is as good as philosophy, but he understands that both are extremely powerful opponents. They are both representative of fundamental human options, and Plato understands very well that they cannot simply disappear. So, when it comes to Sophistry, we certainly have learned that Socrates is not averse to using rhetoric; he borrows the tricks that the Sophist himself would use, and so he defeats Thrasymachus is Book I. And we, of course, know that Socrates is really not averse to using the tools of the poet.

Repeatedly we've seen him tell stories; we've seen him construct images. I suggested in earlier lectures that Books XIII and IX really constitute the story of regime change. Not a logical argument, not a historical analysis, but a story. So Socrates, himself, while criticizing both of his opponents, nonetheless respects both very highly.

I'm finally able to make a very brief suggestion about why Socrates introduces what is, in fact, a bizarre idea, given the rest of the *Republic*, and that is that there is a creative God that creates the forms. Perhaps you can guess what my suggestion is. What he is underlying is the worldview; the view that both the Sophists and the poets hold. It's the view that reality is made. Reality is not seen. Seeing is what the philosopher does. The philosopher sees the truth, the Sophists makes up persuasive arguments, and the poet makes up stories. The enormous emphasis on making in this section, I think, is encapsulated with this otherwise bizarre idea that God himself is created, an idea we do not find anywhere else in the *Republic*.

Lecture Twenty-Two
Book X—The Myth of Er

Scope:

In a move that only Plato is capable of making, he has Socrates, almost immediately after criticizing poetry, telling a poem of his own. Before doing so, he argues that the soul is immortal. Then he tells his own poem about the afterlife. This is the Myth of Er. Er was a warrior who was killed but then returned to life to report on the other world. Socrates's myth gives a detailed description of this cosmic vision and its implications for how human beings should live their lives.

Recall that in Book I, old Cephalus claimed that he would neither cheat nor lie so that when he went to the next life, he would not be punished. The Myth of Er, which concludes the *Republic*, thus comes full circle by returning to the opening theme. Whatever one thinks of Plato's philosophical arguments, there is no denying that he was a masterful writer.

Outline

I. Socrates argues that the soul is immortal (608d–611a).

    A. For every object, there are good and bad things. Good things benefit the object; bad things harm it.

    B. For example, sickness is bad for the body. It will destroy it.

    C. If there were an object that could not be destroyed by its bad thing, it would be indestructible.

    D. What is bad for a soul is injustice.

    E. But injustice, although it makes a soul worse, does not destroy it.

    F. Therefore, the soul is indestructible. It is immortal.

II. The argument is not convincing, but it sets up Socrates's next move: his myth of the afterworld.

III. The Myth of Er can be outlined as follows (614b–621d):

    A. Er was a warrior who returned to life and told what he saw.

B. When someone dies, he goes to the "demonic place" (614c), where he is judged. The "demonic place" is like a waiting room in a train station. Newcomers are there, as well as those who have returned from their 1,000-year journeys.

    1. Those who have been just go upward and to the right and are treated to 1,000 years of "inconceivable beauty" (615a).

    2. Those who have been unjust go downward and to the left and receive 1,000 years of punishment.

    3. Those who are so terribly bad that they are "incurable" receive the punishment of eternal damnation. Tyrants are in this category.

C. After their 1,000-year journeys, the souls are taken on a tour of the cosmos.

    1. They see the eight circular orbits of the heavenly bodies.

    2. They hear the "harmony of the spheres."

    3. They see the geometric beauty of the cosmos.

D. The souls pick their next lives.

    1. There is a lottery to determine the order of their selection.

    2. "Here is the whole risk for a human being" (618c). This is when a human being chooses what kind of life to live.

    3. A man who had lived a decent but non-philosophical life picks first: He chooses the life of a tyrant.

    4. In general, there is an "exchange of evils and goods for most of the souls" (619d). Those who had lived good lives pick bad ones and vice versa.

    5. Odysseus picks last. He chooses "the life of a private man who minds his own business" (620c).

    6. Perhaps Odysseus, who is the most intellectual of Greek heroes, represents the philosopher.

    7. Perhaps Plato's point is that in real life, philosophers must remain private and not get involved in politics. This seems to be the message of Book VI and of Plato's dialogue *The Apology of Socrates*.

E. The myth expresses a view that affirms both freedom and determinism. We choose our own lives but then are "forced" to live with our choices.

IV. The Myth of Er teaches important lessons.

    A. There are two basic possibilities for human beings: philosophy and tyranny.

    B. The *Republic* teaches that philosophy is the best life.

    C. The last words of the *Republic* are: "we shall fare well."

    D. At the heart of the *Republic* is the Platonic conception of the good life, that of the philosopher, one who asks questions without necessarily receiving immediate answers.

Essential Reading:

Plato's Republic, Book X.

Supplementary Reading:

Howland, J. *The Republic: The Odyssey of Philosophy*, pp. 150–160.

Plato. *The Apology of Socrates*.

Roochnik, D. *Beautiful City: The Dialectical Character of Plato's Republic*, pp. 121–128.

Questions to Consider:

1. Do human beings need afterlife myths in order to promote virtue? Or can we try to lead the best possible life even if we think nothing awaits us after we die?

2. Do you think Socrates's treatment of the soul who chose first—the man who had lived a decent but non-philosophical life—is fair? Isn't it possible for a non-philosopher to lead a good life?

3. Can philosophers be political? Or must they always remain private?

Lecture Twenty-Two—Transcript
Book X—The Myth of Er

At the end of the last lecture, I described Plato as something of a trickster, and I want to elaborate a little bit on what I mean by that. I certainly don't mean he's engaged in fun and games and just performing a slight of hand in order to amuse us, far from it. I think what Plato is so good at is throwing a monkey wrench into our expectations. In Book X we've seen him criticize poetry. But then I suggested to you, in fact, much of the *Republic* itself should be construed as a poem—as a story in which characters are imitated— and, in fact, therefore, the *Republic* violates its own stricture.

We will see this pattern dramatically in the last chapter of the *Republic*, the very last section. Immediately after having launched into this extended criticism of poetry, which we discussed in the last lecture, what does Socrates do? I'm sure you can guess. He tells a story; he tells a myth. It's the "Myth of Er." This is a myth which, as we'll see, is an afterworld myth about what happens to us after we die. This is a myth, by the way, which will return us full circle, to the very beginning of the *Republic*. You recall it opens with Cephalus. Cephalus is an old man, but he is not, he says, afraid to die, because he believes he's led a just life and, therefore, won't be punished in the next world. Here at the very end of Book X, through the Myth of Er, Socrates's own poetic creation, we return to that same theme.

What I mean by a trick, in other words, is really a provocation to thought. Again, we're not just being played with, we readers. We're being forced to think hard. The *Republic* doesn't give its secrets easily. We, the readers, have to work hard. Is Plato critical of poetry or is he not? We know good reasons for both answers, and it's exactly that debate that goes inside our own minds as we're reading that, I think, Plato very deliberately is trying to generate. He wants us to be active readers; he wants us to think. The last thing he wants us to do is simply sit passively and write notes and say, well, here's what Socrates says, and it must be true. No, far from it, it's a carefully designed dialogue whose intention is to generate a philosophical response in the reader. So let's move to the Myth of Er.

There's actually a prelude to it. It occurs in line 608d–611a, and this part is not a myth, but an argument. Here, Socrates argues that the soul is immortal. Let me outline the steps of the argument for you, and then we can reflect upon it. Socrates begins by saying, for every object there is a good and a bad thing that relates to it. Illustrated easily with an example: for the body, sickness is bad and health is good. That's the example. Every object has its own bad, its own good. Sickness will destroy the body. Next, Socrates asks a question. What if there were an object that's bad, and the bad thing related specifically to it did not, and could not, destroy its object? This thing would then become indestructible. It would become immortal.

Now, let's focus on the soul. What is the bad for a soul? Well, we've spent a great amount of time in the *Republic* trying to prove that the bad is injustice. But injustice, while it certainly makes a soul worse, doesn't destroy a soul. We have, unfortunately, a vast amount of evidence to demonstrate that. There are plenty of unjust people running around the world. They are damaged by being unjust. Their souls are damaged, but they're still there, they're still alive and kicking. Very often, they occupy positions of political power. What we've discovered, in short, is a thing, namely, the soul, whose bad doesn't destroy it, and therefore, Socrates concludes, the soul is immortal.

As always, I urge you to analyze this argument on your own. You should see if I did a good job in my own analysis. I would suggest that this is not, at least by my reading, a terribly convincing argument. It's an interesting argument, but I personally am not convinced that it irrefutably demonstrates that the soul is immortal. What it does do, however, is set up Socrates's next move, and I've already mentioned what that is. Socrates will next tell a story about the afterworld; what happens to the soul after death. I count that argument that we just outlined to be a kind of prelude to what's really interesting at the end of Book X, and that is the myth itself; the Myth of Er.

The myth takes place between lines 614b–621d. We are now rapidly approaching the very end of Plato's *Republic*. Who was Er? He was a warrior who was killed in battle, but he was allowed to come back to life to report what it was that he had seen in the afterworld. It's a fabulous story, to say the least. Let me try to sketch for you—and it's not a bad exercise to try to draw this yourself, so you can too visualize it—the geography of the afterworld. It's very clearly structured. For someone who apparently hates poetry as much as Plato seems to, this myth is beautifully detailed.

When a soul dies, it's brought down to, what Socrates calls at 614c, the "demonic place." It's a very forbidding title. It means the place of the spirits, the departed, the dead. In this place, which as you'll see as we go further in the story, is probably best imagined as a very crowded railway station or an airport, there are lots and lots of souls milling about. In this place, souls are judged. If they were unjust, they're going to be punished, and they go down, imagine it to be, a tunnel that is at their left. In all of great thinking, left is always bad and right is good. So the bad people go down and to the left. At that point, they embark upon a thousand years of punishment. A thousand years of pain in retribution for the injustice they committed while alive. If the departed is good and had a good, just life while on earth, they are rewarded by going up and to the right. And at that point, they go on another one-thousand-year voyage, and this one is pleasurable; it's blissful.

After the thousand years, they come back. The bad people are coming up and, now, they've made it to the right, and they enter what I'm describing as a waiting room, re-enter it, because this is where they started; and the good people who have gone up and to the right, make their full circle and come back down into the demonic place.

There's only one exception to this rule. It's extremely important, it's the key to my own interpretation of this myth, and that's the tyrant. The tyrant about whom we read so much in Book IX. The tyrant, who is so severely criticized by Socrates, who is said to lead a life that's precisely 729 times worse than the life of the just man. The tyrant naturally goes down to the left for the thousand years of pain, but is not allowed to come back up into the demonic place, into the waiting room. There are big monsters there that keep the tyrant down. And that's where the tyrant stays for eternity. In other words, this is eternal damnation. Tyrants are described as incurable. They're so bad; they'll always be bad. By contrast, a run-of-the-mill bad person, after having gone through the one thousand years of painful punishment, is allowed to return. Presumably this person, as we'll see, has been cured.

What happens next after these one-thousand-year journeys? The souls are taken on a tour. I can imagine them being put on a bus; that's, of course, a silly anachronism, but they are taken on a tour and what they see is miraculous. They see the cosmos itself, they see the eight circular orbits of the heavenly bodies, they hear the harmony of the spheres, and they see, in some way, the geometric beauty of the whole universe, the whole cosmos. They see the world in its complete intelligibility; it's a glorious vision.

What happens next? After going on their tour, these souls have to make a choice—we're headed towards the real crux of the myth—there's a lottery, and the lottery determines the order of selection that each soul will have. What is it that they're selecting? They're selecting the next life they will lead. This is, obviously enough now, a reincarnation myth. So these souls, having undergone one thousand years of either punishment or pleasure, after having gone on the tour of the cosmos, make a choice.

Socrates uses very dramatic language to describe this choice. At 618c he says, "Here is the whole risk for a human being." What I think he means by this, is that everything matters here. What matters for us, and what matters for these departed souls is what kind of life they will choose. I would suggest, and I have suggested several times, this is the main theme of Plato's *Republic*. Yes, it's very much about politics, of course, but at the same time, its fundamental question is exactly the question faced at 618c. What sort of life will you choose?

The person who wins the lottery gets to pick first. This person, it turns out, had lived a very decent life. He was not, however, a philosopher. He was, let's call him, an ordinary good citizen, not a very thoughtful person. Having won the lottery, he's very eager to pick first. What life does he pick? Catastrophic choice, he picks the life of a tyrant. The tyrant always seems so attractive, because, after all, the tyrant has such great power. The tyrant seems to get exactly what he wants; he seems to be able to give orders to everybody. Naturally, he becomes attractive, especially to this first lottery winner who had lived a non-philosophical life.

The point that Socrates makes here is very interesting. What he describes is what he calls an exchange—and I'm referring to 619d—an exchange of evils and goods for most of the souls. Here's what I think he means. Let's recall the mechanics of the myth. If you were a decent person, like the guy who won the lottery, you were rewarded with a thousand years of pleasure. If you were a bad person, you were punished with a thousand years of pain. But what happened to this guy who was rewarded with a thousand years of pleasure? Well, he seems to have been stupefied by the thousand years of pleasure. It made him soft, it made him thoughtless, and it seemingly caused him to make this catastrophic choice of a next life. By contrast, somebody who is bad, having gone through so much punishment, will be so afraid, so cautious, so concerned about not making a bad choice, that it's likely Socrates suggests, they'll make a good choice the second time around. This is what he means at 619d by "an exchange." Those who had good lives end up with bad lives and vice versa. Now, the man who picked first, and picked the life of a tyrant, has done something whose consequences are literally infinite. I'll just remind you of this feature of the myth, which I drew your attention to earlier. The tyrant is counted as someone incurable, and is not allowed back up after the one thousand years of punishment. The tyrant doesn't get another chance. This otherwise pretty decent human being, who made the catastrophic choice of the life of a tyrant, has, in effect, sentenced himself to eternal damnation. We'll reflect on this point a little further in a couple of minutes.

Let's take a look though at one of the most interesting characters who does make what seems to be an excellent choice. This character is Odysseus, famous of course, from Homer's *Odyssey*. Odysseus lost the lottery, he picked last. Nonetheless, he's very pleased when he makes his choice—this is described at 620c—he chooses the life of a private man who minds his own business. Rather surprising choice, but he says this is the choice I would have made had I won the lottery. Now we might just take a step back and think about who Odysseus is as a character in Greek literature, without going into any details about Homer's *Odyssey*. I'll just say this: Odysseus, traditionally in the *Odyssey* and throughout Greek literature, is always conceived of as the intelligent hero. The contrast is always with Achilles, the hero of the *Iliad*, who's the hero of brute force. Odysseus is the master of disguise, he's the master of craft, he's a great liar, and he's a great talker. Odysseus is sometimes described as the hero of words.

I mention this because—and this is an interpretation on my part—it seems to me that Odysseus really stands for the philosopher. If that's the case, and I believe it is, then we are reminded of a theme that we've discussed several times in this course. And that is, that a philosopher must lead a private life. This was an explicit theme in Book VI of the *Republic*; it was a theme that was discussed in Plato's dialogue, the *Apology of Socrates*, which I also mentioned to you.

Again, it's one of those almost tricks that Plato plays on us. We learned about the philosopher king, we've thought that this is the real goal of human aspiration, but in fact, at the very end of the dialogue, we find Odysseus making what seems to be the very best of choices, the choice of a private life.

Let me come back to the issue of tyranny and let me rethink, just slightly, the myth that we've discussed so far. It's a little bit complicated, but not that complicated. I'm sure you can follow it. This myth is actually very surprising in its conclusion it seems to me. Let me explain why. Remember this notion of the exchange of good and evil lives? If you've led a good life, you're rewarded with a thousand years of pleasure, like the guy who won the lottery, but that one thousand years of pleasure actually stupefies you and you end up making a very bad choice second time around. What was the choice that was made the second time around? The life of a tyrant, which means that, that game is over, because the tyrant doesn't get a second chance.

Now let's imagine what happens to the bad person, the unjust person, not the tyrant, but the more ordinary, unjust human being—someone who cheats on her taxes or robs a bank, very bad things to do, but not at the level of being a tyrant. Such a person is punished for a thousand years. But then having been punished so greatly, they're made very disciplined and cautious by the punishment, and therefore, make a good choice second time around. We can then assume that that person is rewarded in their next life with a thousand years of pleasure. Yes, but what did we just learn happens after that one thousand years of pleasure? Stupefaction and a bad choice, a bad choice that eventually leads to the choice of the tyrant.

What I'm suggesting, in short, is that the Myth of Er finally suggests that all human beings will end up being like tyrants and punished for eternity. Might take a thousand years or it might take two thousand years, but it's going to happen. I believe this is the teaching that Socrates implies with this story. There is one exception to this otherwise awful fate: the philosopher, represented by Odysseus.

Socrates makes it clear that somehow—and remember this is only a story, only a myth, so we can't press him to explain exactly how—somehow the philosopher is exempted from this pattern, this looping of one-thousand-year cycles that eventually end up causing someone to be damned for eternity. The philosopher is exempt.

What this suggests is a theme that we have discussed rather often in this course. An implication of the Myth of Er is that there are two basic choices facing humanity: philosophy on the one hand, and tyranny on the other. Now, that doesn't sound immediately plausible. Most of us would think, well, of course there are lots of different kinds of lives, not just two basic choices. But if we remember the basic themes of the *Republic*, we might see why this Myth of Er has this conclusion.

All the way back in the beginning, the first lecture, we discussed some of the historical background that Plato underwent before he wrote the *Republic*, and I made much of the fact that at age 25, he witnessed the Tyranny of the Thirty in the year 404 B.C.E. This made an extraordinary impression on him. He became deeply concerned with the issue of tyranny. He actually knew people who were among those tyrants, these were people who had associated with the historical Socrates and now they were associated with the Tyranny of the Thirty. So, much of his thinking in the *Republic* reflects a preoccupation with the idea of tyranny.

There's another sense in which tyranny is so important to him, and I discussed this in my lecture on the tyrant when we were discussing Book IX of the *Republic*. There is a strange, but unmistakable, similarity between the tyrant and the philosopher. Both of them are characterized by let's call it, extreme eros, extreme ambition, extreme energy, passion, vitality, and aggressiveness. The tyrant expresses his eros in the political sphere. The tyrant has one goal only: maximize power, power, and then more power, that's all I want. The philosopher is equally driven towards his goal or her goal, but the goal is fundamentally different, it's wisdom. But there is a psychological affinity that these two kinds of human beings share. They're both driven by *eros*.

Plato suggests this to us by having Socrates say in the discussion of the tyrant, that eros, from old, has been called a tyrant. I've also suggested to you before that the real target of this dialogue is

Glaucon. Glaucon is a young man, the dialogue you recall in dramatic time, is set somewhere around 410 B.C.E; in actual time it was written around 385 B.C.E. Glaucon is a young man in the year 410 B.C.E. He is, therefore, representative of just the kind of threat that Plato knew would come to pass; young, philosophically minded people who are lured away from philosophy and turn towards politics, turn towards the quest for power. This is precisely what happened to the famous character Alcibiades.

So, it seems to me that one way of understanding the *Republic* as a whole, is to understand it first and foremost, as a dialogue between Socrates and Glaucon, with Socrates trying to seduce Glaucon; not sexually, seduce him to philosophy, to turn him away from politics. I use that phrase "turn him away" deliberately; it's reminiscent of what we discussed when we talked about the Divided-Line, the parable of the cave. Turning around is the fundamental dynamic of philosophical education. It's to turn away from the world of the senses, from the world of the city, and to turn towards the Idea of the Good. I think we can describe Socrates as engaged in the effort to turn Glaucon around.

We've reached the end of Plato's *Republic* with the Myth of Er, and we've concluded that the basic message of the Myth of Er is that one ought to be a philosopher. The very last words of the *Republic* are, "We shall fare well." "We shall do well"—you can translate these last couple of words in a variety of ways—"You shall act well." And these are very strategically located at the end of the dialogue in order to make a point. The whole *Republic* has been about exactly this issue. How does a human being fare well, do well, act well? In other words, what really is the best life a human being can lead?

On the one hand, Plato has a remarkably simple answer to that question, and the answer is, be a philosopher. But at the same time, that's a most puzzling answer. Because, what do we know about philosophy having studied the *Republic*? We know that philosophy is filled with questions. The *Republic* is not easy to understand, to say the least, and not just because it's incredibly complicated. It's not easy to understand because we don't get all the answers to all the questions that are raised in the *Republic*. It's so often a reader of the *Republic* wants to say, give me more, give me more, you're not telling me enough, you're giving me my questions, but you're not giving me the answers to these questions. So, this becomes very peculiar. How can we lead a good life by asking questions?

I think, as peculiar as it may sound, it goes to the heart of the platonic conception of philosophy and, in turn, the platonic conception of the good life. To lead a good life is, in fact, to do just this, to ask questions. There's a very famous line in the *Apology of Socrates*, written by Plato; Socrates there says the unexamined life is not worth living. The only genuinely human form of life is a life of examination, of self-questioning, of self-criticism, of reflection.

Let me put the point in one final way. You've reached the end of the *Republic*; we've read its very last words. What would I recommend you to do next? Start all over. Read it again. We don't have the answers; we've only begun the process of questioning.

Lecture Twenty-Three
Summary and Overview

Scope:

In this lecture, we will review the journey we have taken through the 10 books of Plato's *Republic*. We will produce something of a "highlight film" that includes Socrates's refutation of Thrasymachus, Glaucon's rejection of the city of pigs, the censorship of poetry, the ship of state, the Idea of the Good, the divided line, the parable of the cave, the breakdown of the perfectly just city, the story of the mistaken regimes, the old quarrel between philosophy and poetry, and the Myth of Er. We will try to summarize the great achievements of this extraordinary book.

Outline

I. The *Republic* is structured around several key "interruptions."

    A. Polemarchus "forces" Socrates to stay in the Piraeus (Book I).

    B. Glaucon pressures Socrates to stay in the Piraeus (Book I).

    C. Glaucon and Adeimantus pressure Socrates to do a better job of refuting Thrasymachus (Book II).

    D. Polemarchus and the others force Socrates to return to the issue of sexual relationships (Book V).

    E. The perfectly just city collapses because the rulers cannot calculate the "marriage number" (Book VIII). They fail to regulate sexual relationships with a mathematically based eugenical science.

II. These interruptions tell us much about what kind of book the *Republic* is. It is *dialectical*.

    A. The *Republic* is a giant conversation. It is a dialogue.

    B. It is not an abstract or systematic argument. It is a human attempt to understand the meaning of life.

III. The following is a review of the highlights of the *Republic*.

    A. The refutation of Thrasymachus (Book I) deals with the question of justice and leaves us with an issue of relativism.

B. The city-soul analogy (Book II) implies that humans are naturally political, but the analogy is not fully explained; we are meant to think for ourselves.

C. Justice is seen as "minding one's own business" (Book IV). Bernard Williams offered a telling critique of Plato's concept of the human soul as having a tripartite structure.

D. The three waves (Book V) are the successive conditions upon which the perfectly just city comes into being.

E. The ship of state (Book VI) presents one of the most pessimistic views of politics in history. The person who gains control of the ship is, tragically, not the one who knows how to sail the ship. Perhaps it is not realistic to expect to have a true pilot.

F. The Idea of the Good (Book VI) is not defined by Socrates, who merely makes an analogy with the sun.

G. The divided line (Book VI) is a graphic representation of the struggle of human intellectual progress.

H. The parable of the cave (Book VII) is about education. It requires energy and passion to "fly upwards" toward intellectual progress.

I. Mathematics (Book VII) points mankind in the right direction but is not the ultimate answer in and of itself.

J. The perfectly just city collapses (Book VIII).

K. Socrates is ambivalent in his critique of democracy (Book VIII).

L. The worst criticism of democracy is that it can become a tyranny (Book VIII–IX).

M. The Myth of Er (Book X) implies a surprising affinity between the philosopher and the tyrant.

Essential Reading:

Plato's Republic.

Supplementary Reading:

Roochnik, David. *Beautiful City: The Dialectical Character of Plato's Republic.*

Questions to Consider:

1. Do you think any "highlights" were left off the list presented above?

2. Do you agree with the characterization of the *Republic* as a blend of mathematics and poetry?

Lecture Twenty-Three—Transcript
Summary and Overview

I ended the last lecture with something resembling a joke. I said that the final message of the *Republic* for us readers is we have to begin all over. It's a joke, because we're not going to begin all over, but it was also meant seriously in that I was trying to communicate something about Plato's conception of philosophy itself. The overwhelming message of all of the *Republic*, the Myth of Er in particular, is that this life, the life of the philosopher, the life exemplified by the character Socrates, is the best human life available, and we should all emulate it to the extent that we're capable of doing so. It's a peculiar notion, the notion that philosophy is the life, because philosophy, as construed by Plato at least, seems to be very much a process of asking questions, and not always receiving immediate answers.

Another way I could put this point is to speak about what could be termed, "platonic ethics." Ethics is the study of the good life. Platonic ethics is very simple; lead a philosophical life. But it's also so puzzling, because we typically expect ethics to give us rules or directions, almost a recipe for how to lead a good life; whereas, the platonic move to identify the good life through philosophy itself is to thrust us into a mode of questioning.

We can't start all over with Book I of the *Republic*, but we can look at the *Republic* as a whole. And that's what I'll attempt to do in this lecture, to give an overview of the *Republic*, but a certain kind of overview. One in which I will try to emphasize what I've just been mentioning, the kinds of questions that emerge from this work.

Let me first say a few words about the literary structure of the *Republic*. It seems to me that the best way to think about this book is to understand it as being structured around several key interruptions. That is very interesting, I think, as a literary device. First, interruption is at the very beginning; Polemarchus interrupts Socrates' progress home. He's walking home from the Piraeus, and Polemarchus forces him to stay in the Piraeus, that's of course, from Book I. Glaucon pressures Socrates to stay in the Piraeus, another kind of interruption.

At the beginning of Book II, the parallel is very strong, because here, again, Socrates wishes to go home, but he's not allowed to do so because of the pressure put on him by Glaucon and Adeimantus, Plato's two brothers. They want him, you recall, to do a much better job of actually refuting Thrasymachus. We now begin the train of thought that becomes the rest of the *Republic*, but we began it with an interruption.

In the beginning of Book V, the same pattern repeats itself; Socrates is prepared to go on to the discussion of the unjust regimes—a discussion which eventually takes place in Books VIII and IX—but at Book V, he is not allowed to continue his progress into what then becomes Books VIII and IX. He's forced to return to an issue he has already discussed, namely, the control of women and children, the regulation of sexual relationships.

At the beginning of Book VIII, we have a different kind of interruption. The just city itself, which we've taken such great pains to construct from Book II until the end of Book VII, falls apart. This is not an interruption in the dramatic sense, analogous exactly to the ones I've mentioned, but it is an interruption. It is a breakdown, something happens that's unexpected, the marriage number fails, the rulers are unable to perform what, in fact, is their primary task, and that is to perfect a mathematical science of eugenics and control sexual reproduction. They can't do this, and therefore, the so-called just city falls apart and gives rise to the subsequent regimes, which are less than perfect; the unjust regimes.

Now I mentioned these interruptions, and this conception of the work as a whole, in order to raise the issue of what kind of book the *Republic* is. Above all else, and please do not forget this, the *Republic* is a dialogue, a dialogue between human beings. It is, to use a slightly different word, dialectic. You might remember this word from our discussion of the Divided-Line. Dialectic is there described as the intellectual labor of articulating the world in terms of form. But remember a point I made repeatedly, and that is that the whole notion of a platonic form is a notion that he gets from the "what is it" question that Socrates asks. Socrates asks, what is justice, and this gives rise eventually to the notion of the form of justice, the idea of justice. Socrates asks what is justice, someone answers, Socrates refutes, there's argument against argument, and this is the sense in which dialectic and dialogue go hand in hand.

The *Republic*, in short, is one giant conversation. It's alive. It moves. You and I in our ordinary lives have never had a conversation quite like the *Republic* I'm sure, but we recognize what's going on here, because, in fact, it is rather familiar. If you and I sit down and star to have a long talk—maybe we'll talk about politics, maybe we'll talk about economics, maybe we'll talk about aesthetics, any subject whatsoever—the conversation will take on a life of its own, twists and turns, digressions; this is exactly what goes on in Plato's *Republic*. As a result, let's think about what it's not. What it's not is a systematic theory. It's not anything analogous to a mathematical proof. Plenty of discussions of mathematics in the *Republic*, of course, but the dialogue as a whole is marked more like an ordinary human conversation, than it is to a scientific theory; a mathematical equation. It is a human attempt to understand the meaning of our lives.

Let me turn next to something of a highlight film; a way of reviewing some of the high points of the *Republic*, again, with an eye to the kinds of questions they left us with. Book I, the refutation of Thrasymachus. These were very complicated arguments. We only scratched the surface of them, but when we were studying the refutation of Thrasymachus, I asked you to pay attention to a very minor character. His name was Cleitophon, and he appears only in Book I, utters a few lines, and disappears. If you recall, Thrasymachus's definition of justice was, "It is the advantage of the stronger." Socrates refutes this definition. Cleitophon revises the definition and says justice is not the advantage of the stronger; justice is what the stronger believes to be to his advantage, a subtle shift, but a dramatic one.

Thrasymachus's position can be refuted because Socrates can demonstrate that sometimes rulers make mistakes. I gave the example of tax policy. If I'm a tyrant, I might raise the income tax to a level of 75%. As a result, I think I'll gain a lot of money; it will be to my advantage. It turns out, however, that I've impoverished my citizens and they revolt, and I'm toppled. So, in fact, my law, saying that people must pay 75% to me, has backfired. I made a mistake and this is, finally, a contradiction. Because Thrasymachus on the one hand believes that everybody should obey the law, and on the other hand believes that sometimes the rulers make mistakes. When they do that, they make a law that is disadvantageous.

That's how Socrates refutes Thrasymachus, and that's why Cleitophon changes the definition. Let's change the definition. It's not the advantage of the stronger; it's only what the stronger believes to be to his advantage. Having done that, Cleitophon is eliminating the possibility of mistakes. What he is doing is radicalizing Thrasymachus's relativism. Cleitophon is an extreme relativist. Whatever the ruler thinks is good, will be counted as good.

You recall that I made the point that Socrates does not refute Cleitophon, and perhaps he can't. This is a sense in which that extreme relativism is a position immune to refutation. I think Plato includes Cleitophon in Book I, to raise the issue of relativism in the reader's mind. Can it be refuted? It's such a prevalent position. It's prevalent today; it was prevalent back then. Perhaps it never will be completely refuted, it will always reappear. I'm speaking in an interrogative tone of voice, because that's what Plato leaves us with in Book I.

Book II, the city soul analogy. Like an eye chart, Socrates says, the city is the soul written large. The soul is small and hard to see; fortunately, the city is larger and isomorphic with the soul. And so, we will see justice in the city. Having done so, we can transfer our knowledge to the soul, being confident that city and soul are isomorphic.

What this city-soul analogy implies is that human beings are naturally political. This is in effect, what it means. If the city is no more than a big picture of an individual, then to be a human being is to be in the city, to be political. The Greek word for city, *polis*, that's the sense in which I use the word political. However, I think this is questionable. I think Plato would want us to ask the following: is that true? Are human beings so intimately tied to politics that we couldn't actually be human beings if we were not in a city? I think, finally, Plato would say yes, human beings really are like that, but the city-soul analogy is not fully explained by Socrates, nor is it fully defended. And that lack of a full defense is exactly what I'm trying to highlight. It's left open as something of a question, the burden is placed on the reader. The dialogue is constructed in such a way as to act like a teacher. We are meant to think for ourselves.

In Book IV we learn that justice is famously described as minding one's own business. This applies to both city and soul. In the city, the three classes of the citizens—gold, silver, and bronze—each do their own job. The silver people don't try to do the work of the gold people; the gold people don't do the work of the bronze. When it comes to the individual, we have an analogous, tripartite structure. We have reason corresponding to gold, spirit to silver, and desire to bronze.

I discussed the analogy in some detail, and I mentioned a very famous critic of the analogy, his name was Bernard Williams. Williams asks us to reconsider the city-soul analogy and wonder, does it actually make any sense? Are we really willing to admit that there are three separate parts in the human soul, in the human psyche? If so, we may have a very incoherent picture. This is Williams's critique. Remember, spirit gives assistance to reason and reason gives orders to desire. Desire is not reason. Well, then how does it understand the orders that reason is giving to it? Exactly the same problem would occur on the level of the city when the gold-souled people, corresponding to reason, are giving orders to the bronze-souled people, corresponding to desire. How in the world will they understand the orders unless they themselves are rational? This is a big problem opening up all kinds of issues concerning the nature of the human soul. Does it have parts?

In Book V, we encountered the three "waves." These are the three conditions of the possibility of the coming into being of the perfectly just city. The three waves are women and men must perform all the same tasks, there is sexual communism—in other words, the obliteration of the family. Children are not raised by their biological parents. The third wave is that philosophers must be kings and queens, philosophers must rule. Very puzzling sequence, because the question naturally arises, how does that third wave connect to the first two? The first two are obviously about sex, about gender, about eros; the third wave is about philosophy.

You recall the extraordinary reaction Glaucon has when he hears that philosophers must rule. He says that, well, people are going to go ballistic when they hear this, Socrates. They're going to take their clothes off, pick up whatever happens to be at hand, and attack you. This is, in my view, Plato's way of suggesting to the reader: hey, you better think carefully about this all-together weird idea that philosophers must rule, and you better think about this sequence of three waves, asking yourself, how do they fit together?

In Book VI, we met the ship of state. A very old metaphor, wasn't quite invented by Plato, he certainly made it most famous in Greek literature. The ship of state poses one of the most pessimistic views of politics ever articulated in the history of western political philosophy. You recall the basic notion here is the distinction between the true pilot, the one that could actually sail the ship well, and the pilot who is in charge of the ship and rules the other sailors. There is a distinction between these two people, because the true pilot has to concentrate on the stars and on the sky, studying the stars for navigation, studying the sky for weather patterns. This is how you sailed in antiquity and Plato is playing on that fact. If you're gaze is always upward, then you will pay little attention to what's in front of your nose, the other sailors, and the competition for the rudder, for control of the ship. And as a result, the person who gets control of the ship is precisely and, one might even say, tragically not the person who knows how to sail the ship.

The question raised by this image, the parable, is should we really be so pessimistic about politics, about real-world politics? Do we really want, can we rationally expect, there to be a true pilot of the ship of state? Perhaps that's an unfair expectation to place upon real-world cities.

Let's talk next about the Idea of the Good in Book VI. Surely, this is the highlight of highlights in all of the *Republic*. What's most striking about Socrates' discussion of the Idea of the Good is that he can't tell us what it is and he refuses even to try. Instead, he makes another analogy. The good is like the sun. The sun is an offspring of the good. As the good is to the realm of being, the intelligible realm, so the sun is to the realm of becoming. Two features of the Idea of the Good passage immediately leap out as provocative of questions. First of all, why in the world can't Socrates tell us about the Idea of the Good directly? Why does he have to engage in this imagery of the child or offspring of the good? Second, even if we allow him his image of the sun as the offspring of the good, we need to remember a simple but significant fact about the sun, it cannot be seen. If you look at the sun, you burn your eyes. You can feel the warmth of the sun, see its reflection; you can know its effects, but you can't see it directly, except in very brief glimpses. I think this is, as usual, very deliberate on Plato's part. He's suggesting, I believe, that we'll never get a full understanding of the Idea of the Good, the supreme ontological and epistemological principle of his entire philosophical conception. It's a rather disheartening notion; on the one hand, we're never going to understand everything. We might, however, get a glimpse once in a while; just as we once in a while get a glimpse of the sun, and that might be enough to nourish us, so that we can continue our quest to our understanding even better.

Next topic is the Divided-Line. Surely, in the history of philosophy, at least in my experience, there is no more condensed economical passage available. In the space of only a few lines, Socrates sketches, literally in the sand at his feet, a picture of all of reality. It's a remarkable achievement, the Divided-Line. The basic thrust of it is that we start at the bottom with images, we work our way up the sensible things, to mathematical objects, to forms, and then, one hopes, to the Idea of the Good. The very key idea that I emphasized, and would repeat, is that the Divided-Line requires us, we philosophical students, we philosophical leaders, to turn around. What most people do is they reach that level of mathematics on the Divided-Line, and then go back down. Why is that? Because Plato understood exactly how powerful mathematics could be. It's as if Plato could predict Galileo and Newton, the great mathematical physicists of modern times.

He understood that mathematics was a tool and was terribly useful as a result. I described this as the temptation or the lure of intellectual gravity. Mathematics, in a way, invites us to go back down into the sensible world and manipulate things, because we now are equipped with this remarkable tool. The thrust of the Divided-Line quite to the contrary is, reverse direction, don't go down; continue to go up, that's exactly the same message we repeatedly hear in the parable of the cave in Book VII. Education is a turning around, a liberation, and a movement towards the sun. It is painful, it is difficult, and what it requires, as I suggested throughout this course, above all else, is it requires energy. It requires passion; it requires eros. In order to reverse direction on the Divided-Line, one must defy intellectual gravity. One has to sprout wings and fly upwards. That's an image, by the way, that I just borrowed from another dialogue by Socrates called the *Phaedrus*, where the soul is described as having wings. It naturally wants to go up. Going up is the direction that is quintessentially platonic.

We discussed in Book VII the role of arithmetic, indeed of mathematics in general. This is a very important section, I think, especially for us living as we do, in a highly computerized, digitalized world. Mathematics, one could say, is the language of our time. We think of the universe now, as it seems, as consisting of zero and one. Zero and one are the two essential ingredients of the digital world.

I think Plato would criticize us in the following way. He is a great lover of mathematics. He is a great admirer of mathematics, but he thinks that mathematics has only limited value. You recall the description of arithmetic in Book VII. It's a very nice thing to study, but it's nice because it turns the soul around from becoming to being. It points us in the right direction. Numbers are stable, intelligible; they are a lot like forms. That's what's good about them, they're not so valuable in and of themselves, they're valuable for what they produce in the student of mathematics, which is a reorienting, a turning. Again, I think this is a very useful lesson for us living in a world in which many people believe mathematics is the queen of the sciences—not for Plato.

This point is reiterated in the failure of the marriage number at the beginning of Book VIII, which I've already discussed in this lecture. This is one of those interruptions I pointed to. It is a failure of mathematics to capture the human erotic impulse, to control it with efficiency. Can't be done, suggests Plato, thereby opening up the door to a whole series of questions. If mathematics can't understand the human soul, what can?

One of the most vicious criticisms of democracy ever articulated is found in Book VIII of the *Republic*, and we discussed it at length. Plato is infamous for being a critic of democracy, a system we hold very dear. What I suggested to you at the time, and will now reiterate, is that while on the one hand Socrates is very serious in his criticisms of democracy, at the same time, he is surprisingly ambivalent. You recall, perhaps, what he said, which I'll paraphrase, perhaps it is necessary if one wants to engage in the activities we have just been now engaged in, to live in a democracy. What that suggested to me is that philosophy itself, which is of course, what they have been engaged in, is nourished by a democracy. In a democracy there is freedom, in a democracy there is privacy, there is no compulsion to be political; as a result, one can pursue one's own intellectual projects.

The worst criticism of democracy is that it eventually becomes the tyranny, and there is no regime worst than the tyranny, we discussed that in our lectures on Books VIII and IX. But I also suggested to you then that this is a questionable move that Socrates makes, because in a very surprising fashion, there is this almost disturbing affinity between the tyrant and the philosopher. This became a major point of emphasis in my reading of the Myth of Er in Book X.

Again, these are surprises; and with these surprises, Plato is prompting us, the careful attentive reader, the reader who is active rather than passive, to pursue these surprises, to ask these questions, and to try to answer them for ourselves.

Lecture Twenty-Four
The Legacy of Plato's *Republic*

Scope:

Alfred North Whitehead once said, "The safest general characterization of the European philosophical tradition is that it consists of a series of footnotes to Plato." The last lecture in this course will be a brief look at some of these "footnotes." We will begin with Aristotle's critique of the *Republic* found in his book *The Politics*. We will then turn to Machiavelli's *The Prince*, Hobbes's *Leviathan*, and John Stuart Mill's *On Liberty* to see a thoroughly modern, thoroughly anti-Platonic view of politics. We will discuss the views of Immanuel Kant in order, once again, to see conceptions of the moral and political life that are radically at odds with what Socrates proposes in the *Republic*. Finally, we will mention Karl Marx's work in order to see a view that is not entirely opposed to what Socrates proposes.

It is a wild exaggeration to call all these great thinkers mere "footnotes to Plato," but it is nonetheless true that their works can all enter into a dialogue with the *Republic*. It is for this reason that the claim was made, in Lecture One of this course, that the *Republic* is the most influential work in the history of Western political philosophy.

Outline

I. Alfred North Whitehead once said, "The safest general characterization of the European philosophical tradition is that it consists of a series of footnotes to Plato."

    A. This means that subsequent philosophers took up the questions Plato first raised.

    B. The history of philosophy continues a dialogue that commenced with Plato.

II. Consider the following examples:

    A. Aristotle's *Politics* became one of the most influential books in the Middle Ages.

        1. Aristotle studied with Plato for 20 years (367–347).

2. In Book II of the *Politics*, he criticizes the *Republic*.

3. Socrates's perfectly just city is too rigidly organized. It is too much of a unity and, thus, not a real city.

4. The abolition of private property would have counterproductive results. Citizens would become apathetic.

5. Aristotle warns that political ideology can lead to huge problems.

6. He proposes a blend of democracy and oligarchy.

B. Machiavelli's *The Prince* was tremendously influential during the Renaissance.

1. Niccolo Machiavelli (1469–1527) is often counted as the first modern political theorist.

2. He was a "realist" who believed that idealism is disastrous.

3. A successful ruler must be willing to be flexible, rather than rigidly moralistic. A successful ruler must be willing to be evil if necessary.

4. His position is not unlike that of Thrasymachus: The end justifies the means.

C. Hobbes's *Leviathan* was the first work of political philosophy that tried to take account of the "new science" of mathematical physics.

1. Thomas Hobbes (1588–1679) is usually counted as the founder of English moral and political philosophy.

2. He was a materialist.

3. In the state of nature, life is "solitary, poor, nasty, brutish and short." There is a war of all against all.

4. It is rational, therefore, for human beings to give up some of their rights in order to create a state that will offer them security.

5. His position is not unlike that offered by Glaucon at the beginning of Book II, when he suggests that justice is a good, not desirable for itself but only for its consequences.

D. Kant's *Groundwork of the Metaphysics of Morals* is one of the most famous books in the history of moral philosophy.

1. Immanuel Kant (1724–1804) was arguably the most influential philosopher of the modern age.

2. He developed the concept of the *categorical imperative*, an absolute demand for moral action.

3. He argued that it was never morally justifiable to lie. He would have strongly opposed Socrates's noble lie.

4. He argued that human autonomy and dignity must be respected. He was an egalitarian.

5. Kantian ethics is fundamentally opposed to the basic principles of Socrates's just city.

E. Mill's *On Liberty* is a crucial text for modern "liberalism."

1. John Stuart Mill (1806–1873) is often thought to be the greatest British philosopher of the 19th century.

2. In *On Liberty*, he argues that the only justification for the state to restrict the freedom of an individual is to prevent harm to others.

3. For Mill, if the law doesn't prohibit it, then an individual can do whatever he wants. For Plato, the individual can do only what the law tells him to do.

4. Mill justifies his "liberalism" by arguing that the liberation of individual talents will bring great progress.

5. His position could not be further from that embraced by Socrates's perfectly just city.

6. In *On Utilitarianism*, Mill argues that it is wrong to lie. Although lies achieve short-term goals, they create long-term instability.

7. Mill would object to Socrates's noble lie.

F. Marx's *Capital* was notorious in the 20th century.

1. Karl Marx (1818–1883) is the major source of inspiration for all forms of modern social radicalism.

2. He argued for the elimination of private property. Here, he would be in agreement with Socrates's treatment of the guardians.

3. He argued for the abolition of classes. Here, he would strongly disagree with Socrates's division of all the citizens into three separate classes.

4. The failure of Marxist experiments in the Soviet Union and elsewhere is perhaps predicted by Socrates's descriptions of the breakdown of the perfectly just city in Book VIII of the *Republic*.

III. It is absurd to label these great thinkers "footnotes to Plato."

    A. They do, however, all take up themes that Plato first explored.

    B. Even if one disagrees with much in the *Republic*, it is impossible to deny how rich it is.

Essential Readings:

Honderich, Ted, ed., *The Oxford Companion to Philosophy*.

Supplementary Readings:

Cropsey, Joseph, and Leo Strauss, eds. *History of Political Philosophy*.

Questions to Consider:

1. Marxism seems to have been totally discredited by the events of the 20th century. Do you think the comparison between Socrates's ideal city and Marx's conception of communism is apt? If so, does the 20th century discredit the *Republic*?

2. Machiavelli is famous for being a "realist" who thinks idealism gets political leaders into trouble. Is Plato an idealist or a realist?

Lecture Twenty-Four—Transcript
The Legacy of Plato's *Republic*

My last lecture on Plato's *Republic* will not be about Plato at all. It will be, instead, a tribute to Plato. Because what I plan to do in this lecture is discuss his influence on the subsequent history of western political philosophy.

The 20th century philosopher, Alfred North Whitehead once said, "The safest general characterization of the European philosophical tradition, is that it consists of a series of footnotes to Plato." This is a very famous idea that the rest of the history of philosophy is no more than footnotes to Plato. On the one hand, this is so obviously preposterous that it's easy to dismiss, for it suggests that all the remaining philosophers in the history of the West added nothing new, made no real progress. They simply were tinkering with something Plato had already thought about, and I certainly don't think that's the case. I think many philosophers have said many new and interesting things after Plato.

But there is a sense in which Whitehead, I believe, is correct. This is the sense that I was trying to emphasize in the previous lecture. Plato didn't give us all the answers, but he may have asked all the questions. He got a whole process of thought into motion; this process subsequently became the history of philosophy. Again, I don't want to get too carried away with my enthusiasm for Plato, perhaps that's what happened to Whitehead. But I am, nonetheless, very confident that there is a chunk of truth in Whitehead's characterization, and that's what I would like to illustrate to you in this lecture.

I'm going to discuss a very small sample of political philosophers and try to show you how they were responding to questions that Plato asked. It's not going to be necessary for me to prove to you that, in each and every case, these philosophers were actually even reading Plato, not to say actually responding directly and literally to him. I don't have to prove that. What I am going to try to show you is that they are participating in a conversation whose origin is the *Republic*.

Let's start with Aristotle. He was Plato's student. He came down from Macedonia in the north and he studied in Plato's Academy from 367–347 B.C.E. He began when he was 17 years old and he left when he was 37, at the death of Plato. Clearly, Plato was the monumental influence on Aristotle, but like every good student, Aristotle not only absorbed the lessons of his teacher, he also criticized. Let's consider a book he wrote titled the *Politics*, a book that became hugely influential, especially in the Middle Ages when Aristotle was a dominant force in European civilization. The curriculum of the first European universities, which arose in the Middle Ages, was in fact established by Aristotle.

In Book II of the *Politics*, he explicitly criticizes the *Republic*. Let's just look at a couple of points he makes. He says that, for example, Socrates' just city is too unified. You recall that a major objective of the legislation and the regulation that Socrates proposes is to foster unity among the cities. He used a phrase, such as the community of pains and pleasures. If another citizen feels a pain, I should feel a pain; that's how close the link should be between citizens. You recall the noble lie. The noble lie tells us that all citizens have the same parent; the parent is the city. We should all, therefore, be patriots, literally meaning treating the city as our parent. We should all act as if we were siblings, brothers and sisters; we have the same parent. This, of course, is a major emphasis in the *Republic*, and it's exactly what Aristotle criticizes. He says a city can't be like a family. That's in essence what Socrates proposed with the noble lie, is that the city become one big family.

Aristotle is a very patient and methodical observer of reality and he notices that cities are really quite different from families. There can be intimacy and solidarity in the family. It may, however, be a big mistake to attempt to generate such intimacy and proximity in the city. Another way to put this point, by being a bit more specific, is to remind ourselves of the abolition of private property that is focused, in the *Republic*, on the guardians. They don't have private homes, they don't have any private property, nor do they even have a private family; the city is their family.

Aristotle argues in Book II of the *Politics*, that this is a very counterproductive measure. He makes and argument that will sound very familiar today. He says, look, people really only care about property when it belongs to them. If I own my own house, I'll take care of it. If I don't own it, then I might not take care of it. This is a very familiar debate that we have had in American politics for many, many years. Every time that government takes over a certain function in the lives of citizens, some people react by saying no, government shouldn't do this because if government intrudes, then citizens become apathetic; they're not nearly as productive, they're not as energized. What really gets people active and productive is owning their own property. This is a debate, we're having it now, and Aristotle had it with Plato in his criticism of the *Republic*. For me, this is a perfect example of what it means to say that the history of political philosophy is like a footnote to the *Republic*. Plato didn't answer the question definitively—no one reads the *Republic* and says, aha, I have the answer to every political question—but a question is set into motion. Aristotle continues the conversation.

Here's another point Aristotle makes, very much a follow-up to the *Republic*. Aristotle warns us, don't be too idealistic when you approach politics. Politics belongs to the real world, and if you are obsessed with your philosophical, theoretical ideal, you might end up in big trouble. So what Aristotle does is spend a lot of time, this largely takes place in Books III, IV, and V of his *Politics*, articulating what is the best possible city. Aristotle is a man of the real world; Plato, at least in Aristotle's eyes, is too much of an idealist, and what Aristotle proposes, is a blend of democracy and oligarchy. This is his recipe for what would be the best possible city. Very familiar ideas, democracy and oligarchy; Plato didn't quite invent them, but he certainly was the first to exploit them so carefully in the *Republic*.

Aristotle has real appreciation for democracy, but he's worried about the possibility of mob rule. He doesn't think there should be too much direct democracy. The people—the majority, the *dêmos*—are very good at making certain kinds of decisions, but not all decisions. So, we need a little bit of oligarchy—ruled by the few, the *ligoi*—to balance out the democracy. If that sounds familiar, it should. It resembles some of the ideas held by the founding fathers, who in the creation of our own American system, built into it, non-democratic features, precisely to counterbalance the democratic features of the political regime. Again, these are ideas that have been in play now for centuries, Aristotle versus Plato, echoing all the way until our own time.

Let me jump ahead by centuries and talk about the great political philosopher, Niccolo Machiavelli. He lived 1469–1527, and here, of course, I'm using dates from the common area. He wrote a very famous book titled the *Prince*, a book that has been tremendously influential. Like Aristotle, Machiavelli was a realist. He was a realist with a vengeance. Machiavelli believed that nothing could be worse than idealism, especially in politics. And here's, I think, what he has in mind.

Let's imagine a prince, and Machiavelli is writing at a time in Italy that actually resembles the ancient Greeks, whom we discussed. It was a time not of Italy as a country, it was a time of small city-states like Venice, Machiavelli's own city of Florence, Pisa; each city was run by a prince. Machiavelli's book the *Prince* is addressed to a would-be ruler of a city-state. And, once again, his main point, which sounds very surprising perhaps, is don't be too idealistic, don't be too moral. One of the things a ruler has to learn, according to Machiavelli, is how to be cruel, how, even, to be evil. It sounds horrifying.

His point is that a ruler who is so obsessed with being good and being moral will be very rigid and will not be able to anticipate all the contingencies and problems and realities of real-life politics. Machiavelli is said to have invented *Realpolitik*. Politics that takes its bearings not from some theoretical structure like Plato's *Republic*, but from the real world of blood and battles, political in fighting, self-interest. He was the expert at that.

Let me tell you one of the questions that Machiavelli asks and then proposes an answer to, which I think is very revealing of his attitude towards politics in general. He asks the question, should a ruler be loved or feared? Well, best of all, would be both. But what if you couldn't have both? What's the best way to rule? Is it by love or by fear? Machiavelli argues, it's by fear; and here's why. Love is dependent on someone else. I may try to get you to love me, a ruler may try to get his subjects to love him, but people are very fickle, and I might fail. Whether I'm loved or not, is up to you. And that's a bad situation, says Machiavelli, for a prince to be in. Fear, however, is up to me. If I inflict severe bodily harm on some of the citizens and make it very clear that I'm willing to do so again, I think I can get my people to be afraid of me; that's the effective tool of rule.

Another way to put this point—and Machiavelli is famous for this position—is that "the end justifies the means." The end of the prince, the goal of the prince's work, is to achieve political power, political stability, and whatever it takes to achieve this, whatever means are necessary to achieve this, are acceptable to Machiavelli—the end justifies the means.

This reminds me of Thrasymachus in Book I of the *Republic*. Indeed, it sounds like precisely his praise of injustice. Did Machiavelli read Book I of the *Republic*? I honestly don't know. But I am certain that he is continuing this conversation that Plato began when he had this character Thrasymachus raise the possibility that a life of injustice is superior, more powerful, mightier, and freer than a life of justice.

I turn next to Thomas Hobbes who lived 1588–1679, and was the author of the book *Leviathan*. Hobbes is usually counted as the founder of English moral and political philosophy. He was very much under the influence of the physicist Galileo. He was the first philosopher in modern times who tried to combine the mathematical physics of Galileo with political philosophy. He was a materialist. A materialist is someone who believes that reality itself is constituted by nothing except matter or, to be slightly more precise, nothing except atoms and the void through which the atoms move.

Saying that suggests immediately, of course, that he was an anti-Platonist. Plato believes that the forms are real, the Idea of the Good is real, and neither the forms nor the Idea of the Good are material. Once again, we have a basic disagreement. Hobbes knew very well that he was criticizing ancient philosophers. He devotes a whole chapter, chapter 46 of his book *Leviathan*, to critique ancient philosophy, specifically on this issue of immaterial substance, something real that's not material.

Hobbes was also what's known as a social contract theorist. A social contract theorist is someone who believes that human beings originally, in what came to be known as the "state of nature," were not political. And according to Hobbes, in the state of nature, before there was government state politics in the state of nature, human beings were completely free. This sounds very good, except for the fact that in the state of nature, because we were so free, one of the things we did in the state of nature, was go after other people's property. The state of nature, in fact, as Hobbes describes it, was a war of all against all. Everybody is competing against everybody else, trying to outdo everybody else. There is no government, there are no inhibitions, and there are no constraints on human acquisitiveness or human freedom.

The life in the state of nature, according to Hobbes in a famous phrase, is solitary, poor, nasty, brutish, and short. Therefore, what people did—and this, of course, is a theoretical principle, it's not a historical fact—what people did was engage in a social contract. They made a kind of deal. They created a government and the government would restrict their freedom, and this is a loss. The gain, and the contract implies loss and gain, the gain was security. In the state of nature, I always had to be afraid of you, because there was nothing to stop you from punching me in the nose and taking my property. One can't do that when there's a government. The government puts a clamp on our behaviors and doesn't allow us to do everything we want to do. Again, there is loss and gain. It's rational, in short, for human beings to give up some of their freedoms in exchange for security.

I hope that sounds a bit familiar. It should remind you of what Glaucon says at the beginning of Book II of the *Republic*, because there he suggests that justice is not good for itself. You recall, perhaps, that Glaucon identifies three different kinds of good things. Some good things are good for themselves, some good things are not good for themselves, but bring good consequences—an example would be a very bad tasting medicine that has a good effect— and some good things are good for themselves and for their consequences. And there, Glaucon says, most people believe that justice is number two. It's not good in itself; it's only good for its consequences. That's a version of the social contract theory.

Not only Hobbes, but John Locke, Rousseau, John Rowels, these are famous names in the history of social contract theory. They can all be construed without too much exaggeration, as footnotes to Book II of Plato's *Republic*.

Let me mention next Immanuel Kant, 1724–1804. Kant was almost certainly the greatest single philosopher of the modern age. He was surely the greatest single moral philosopher in modernity. He wrote a book titled the *Groundwork of* the *Metaphysics of Morals*, which is still taught today. It's taught in almost every introductory ethics course in almost every American university.

Kant developed the concept of what he called the "categorical imperative." Without going into any detail, what the categorical imperative is, is an absolute demand for moral action. A categorical imperative is categorical, meaning no ifs, ands, or buts. So, the famous example that Kant gives of the categorical imperative is the prohibition against lying. One should not lie under any circumstances, even circumstances as dire as the one that he imagines.

Imagine there was a murderer on the loose, and he was chasing somebody. This person came to your house and said, please, give me shelter. Okay, you would say, you can hide in my basement. A few minutes later the murderer knocks on your door, and says, is there somebody hiding in your basement? This will not sound too plausible, but Kant would say you are not morally permitted to lie, even in those circumstances. That, again, is what is meant by the categorical imperative. It's an absolute demand on moral action. I mention the example, of course, because it puts us into conversation with Socrates.

For Socrates, lying goes to the heart of politics. There could be, Socrates suggests, no city that didn't lie. This is the famous noble lie. And Socrates tells other lies. Perhaps you'll recall that in the attempt to regulate sexual reproduction, he fabricates a lottery. He tells people it's a matter of chance, whereas, in fact, it's a matter of design.

Kant was a great believer in human dignity and individual autonomy. Kant was an egalitarian. He believed that every human being, simply by virtue of the fact that he or she was human, deserved respect; deserved to be treated with dignity. I would remind you, in this context, of Socrates' medical ethics. I made much of this, precisely in order to suggest the kind of contrast with a philosopher like Kant. For Socrates, my example, perhaps you recall, was of a 90-year-old man in the hospital. For Socrates, all human beings are not created equal; all human beings do not deserve an equal amount of respect. The 90-year-old in the hospital, perhaps, says Socrates, shouldn't even be given healthcare because it's a drain on resources; resources that could be rationally allocated somewhere else. For example, the treatment of a healthy person who suffers a broken arm or has a virus, that's a good use of medical resources, because such a person gets back to work. The 90-year-old is never going back to work. To put it very cruelly, let's let that man die. That's the Socratic motto. Kant would absolutely disagree. Again, we have a conversation.

John Stuart Mill lived from 1806–1873 and he's often thought to be the greatest British philosopher of the 19th century. He wrote many books on many subjects. I'll mention only one, *On Liberty*. This is the crucial text for modern liberalism. Liberalism is a bit of a dangerous word, because the way we use liberal in contemporary political discourse is not what someone like Mill had in mind. A liberal, in Mill's sense, is someone who identifies liberty as the fundamental principle of political and moral life. According to Mill, the only justification for restricting the liberty of anyone is to prevent that person from harming or restricting the liberty of someone else. These are very familiar ideas to us.

It goes without saying that these ideas are the antithesis of the *Republic*. The *Republic* is not a place that values liberty in this sense. To use another word, freedom; the *Republic* is not a place where freedom is a paramount concern.

Let me put the point in the following way. According to Mill, if the law doesn't say you can't do it, then it's okay to do it. I can do anything I want, as long as the law doesn't prohibit it. For Plato, it's quite different. I think the Platonic response would be, you can only do what the law tells you to do. This is a basic difference, indeed. Mill would justify his liberalism by arguing that the liberation of individual talents leads to great progress, and that position could not be further from the one embraced by Socrates.

Mill, in another book entitled *Utilitarianism*—also with Kant, although for different reasons—argues that lying is just fundamentally wrong. Mill argues not by means of a categorical imperative, but in terms of the consequences of lying. If I lie to you and you discover that I've lied to you, our relationship will be plagued by distrust and insecurity, and that's a bad thing. And that's why, according to Mill, we shouldn't lie. So, once again, although he disagrees with Kant's reasoning, he joins Kant in criticizing Socrates' noble lie.

Karl Marx lived from 1818–1883. He was the major source of inspiration for all forms of modern social radicalism, especially in the 20th century. I'll mention just a couple of points that make contact with Plato's *Republic*. Marx was famous for arguing on behalf of the abolition of private property. You recall, of course, that this is a feature of the life of the guardians; they have no private property. For much the same reason, Marx would deny private property in order to foster social solidarity, to foster communism; we live in common.

A disagreement with Socrates would be that Marx also advocated the abolition of classes and class distinctions. By contrast, of course, Socrates is adamant about keeping the city stratified: gold, silver, and bronze. Again—and I'm certain Marx did read Plato, I'm not certain that he was explicitly commenting on the *Republic* when he wrote *Capital*, but he certainly knew Plato was in the background— he's in a dialogue with Plato.

On the one hand, to go back to Whitehead's quote, it's absurd to label these great thinkers as mere footnotes to Plato. They do, however, all take of themes that Plato first explored. And this is, I hope, a fitting way for us to end this course, with disagreement and with dialogue. We've just seen how this very small sampling of western political philosophers disagrees, takes up issues against Plato's *Republic*, but in doing so, they bring it to life. And that has been my own objective in teaching this course, which I hope you've enjoyed.

Timeline

B.C.E.

750–700 ....The approximate dates of Homer and Hesiod.

585 ....Thales predicts a solar eclipse. The beginning of Western philosophy.

508 ....Cleisthenes enacts basic reforms, which start to move Athens toward democracy.

490 ....Greeks defeat Persians at the Battle of Marathon.

480 ....Greeks defeat Persians at Salamis.

478 ....Formation of the Delian League, an alliance of Greek city-states dominated by Athens.

469 ....Birth of Socrates.

469 ....Pericles ascends to power in Athens.

456 ....Death of Aeschylus, the tragedian.

432 ....Parthenon completed.

431 ....Beginning of the Peloponnesian War.

429 ....Death of Pericles.

429 ....Birth of Plato.

406 ....Death of Sophocles, the tragedian.

406 ....Death of Euripides, the tragedian.

405–404 ....Athenians lose a decisive battle to the Spartans at Aegospotami. Restoration of Athenian democracy. End of the Peloponnesian War.

404–403 ....Tyranny of the Thirty in Athens.

399 ....Socrates executed.

388 ....Plato makes his first visit to Sicily, where he befriends Dion, a relative of Dionysius I, the ruler of Syracuse.

386 ....Plato founds his school in Athens, known as the Academy.

385 ....Death of Aristophanes, the comic poet.

368 ....Aristotle enters the Academy.

367 ....Dionysius I dies and is succeeded by Dionysius II. Plato visits and tries to educate Dionysius II. He fails.

348 ....Death of Plato.

322 ....Death of Aristotle.

Glossary

Aristokratia: "aristocracy." Literally, the "rule of the best." The perfectly just city, ruled by philosophers, is meant to be such a regime.

Aristos: "best."

Arithmos: "number." Root of our word *arithmetic*. The crucial first subject studied by the philosopher-kings.

Dêmokratia: "democracy." Literally, the "rule of the people." Plato is famously critical of democracy.

Dêmos: "the people."

Dialetikê: "dialectic." This is the ultimate subject studied by Plato's philosopher-kings. It is a study of the formal structure of all reality.

Dianoia: "thought." The cognitive activity found at the second highest stage of the divided line. It is responsible for the apprehension of mathematical objects.

Eidos: "form." Derived from the Greek verb *idein*, which means "to see," *eidos* literally means the "look" of a thing. It is a technical term for Plato and refers to the intelligible objects that give reality its structure.

Eikasia: "imagination." This is the cognitive activity found at the bottom of the divided line. It is responsible for the apprehension of images.

Eikones: "images." The root of our word *icon*.

Elenchus: "refutation." Socrates was famous for refuting people by showing how their positions contained contradictions.

Epistêmê: "knowledge" or "science." Root of our word *epistemology*, which means "the study of knowledge."

Eros: "love, desire." A crucial concept for Plato. The philosopher is an erotic person because he or she loves wisdom.

Idea: "idea" or "form." Synonymous with *eidos*, it is also derived from the verb *to see*.

Kalon: "beautiful" or "fine." The Greek word has both aesthetic and moral connotations.

Kratê: "power, rule." The root of the suffix of such words as *democracy* and *aristocracy*.

Noêsis: "intellection." The highest cognitive activity, found at the top segment of the divided line. It is responsible for the apprehension of Forms.

Oligarchia: "rule by the wealthy few." One of the "mistaken" regimes Socrates describes.

Oligos: "few." Root of the word *oligarchy*, rule by the wealthy few.

Philosophia: "love of wisdom."

Pistis: "trust." The second-to-lowest cognitive activity found on the divided line. It is responsible for the apprehension of sensible objects.

Polis: "city." Root of our word *political*. The Greek *polis* was a "city-state," an independent and self-sufficient political entity.

Politeia: "republic, regime." The organizing principle of a *polis*.

Psuchê: "soul." Root of our word *psychology*, the study of the soul.

Sophia: "wisdom." Root of our word *philosophy*, the love of wisdom.

Technê: "art, craft." Root of our words *technical* and *technology*.

Timê: "honor." What a spirited man such as Glaucon desires.

Timokratia: "rule by those who love honor." One of the "mistaken regimes" Socrates discusses.

To Agathon: "the Good." The supreme principle of Platonic philosophy. Also called "the Idea of the Good."

To On: "being." Root of our word *ontology*, the study of being.

Biographical Notes

Adeimantus: Brother of Plato, major character in the *Republic*. His dates are unknown, but he is presumed to be older than both Plato and Glaucon.

Aeschylus (525–456): The first great tragic poet and a loyal Athenian patriot.

Aristophanes (455–386): The greatest Athenian comic poet. In his play "The Assembly of Women," proposals are made concerning the role of women that are similar to ones made in the *Republic*.

Aristotle (384–322): One of the greatest philosophers in Western history. He came from his home in Stagira, near Macedon, to study with Plato for 20 years, then founded his own school in Athens.

Cephalus: A wealthy arms manufacturer who migrated to the Piraeus from Syracuse. The conversation of the *Republic* takes place in his home.

Cleitophon: Appears briefly in Book I of the *Republic*. Plutarch reports that he was initially an associate of Socrates who eventually rejected the philosopher's influence. Plato wrote a short dialogue titled *The Cleitophon*.

Dion (408–354): Brother-in-law of Dionysius I, the ruler of Syracuse. He was impressed by Plato when the philosopher visited in 389 and tried to make Dionysius II a philosopher-king.

Dionysius I (430–367): Ruler of Syracuse.

Dionysius II (397–336): Eldest son of Dionysius I. Plato's attempt to educate him and mold him into a philosopher-king failed.

Euripides (480–406): Athenian tragic playwright of the 5th century.

Glaucon: Plato's brother and, after Socrates, the major character of the *Republic*.

Gorgias (483–376): From Leontini, one of the earliest and greatest Greek Sophists. He taught rhetoric. Thrasymachus seems to embrace some of his views in Book I of the *Republic*.

Hesiod (wrote around 700): After Homer, the second greatest epic poet of ancient Greece. His most important work is the *Theogony*, which is heavily censored by Socrates in Book II of the *Republic*.

Homer (wrote some time around 700): The greatest of the ancient Greek epic poets. His *Odyssey* and *Iliad* were fundamental in the development of Western literature. His work is censored by Socrates in Book II of the *Republic*.

Isocrates (436–338): Prominent and influential Athenian rhetorician. His school in Athens was the chief rival to Plato's Academy.

Pericles (495-429): The most influential Athenian statesman during the greatest period in Athenian history. Architect of the Peloponnesian War.

Plato (429-347): Great Athenian philosopher. Son of rich and powerful parents. Was influenced by Socrates. Created his own school, "The Academy." Wrote approximately 25 dialogues, and 13 letters. Arguably the most influential philosopher in Western history.

Polemarchus: Son of Cephalus. Executed by the Tyranny of the Thirty in 404.

Protagoras (c. 490–420): From Abdera, the first of the Greek Sophists. Thrasymachus, in Book I of the *Republic*, seems to share his relativistic position.

Socrates (469–399): Plato's philosophical inspiration. He was famous for interrogating his fellow Athenians by asking them questions, such as "What is justice?" He was executed by the Athenian democracy in 399, probably because the citizens associated him with the Tyranny of the Thirty.

Sophocles (496–406): The great tragic playwright of 5th-century Athens.

Thales (625?–547?): Widely considered to be the first philosopher in the Western tradition. Legend has it that he correctly predicted an eclipse in 585.

Thrasymachus (wrote 430–400): A professional teacher of rhetoric. He is featured in Book I of the *Republic* as Socrates's Sophistic opponent *par excellence*.

Bibliography

Essential Reading:

There are many fine translations of Plato's *Republic*. The most literal and the one cited throughout this course is:

Plato's Republic. Translation by Allan Bloom. New York: Basic Books, 1969.

Other good translations are:

Plato: The Republic. Translation by T. Griffith. Cambridge: Cambridge University Press, 2000. This book has a good introduction and glossary of terms.

Plato's Republic. Translation by G. Grube and C. Reeve. Indianapolis: Hackett, 1994.

Plato: The Republic. Translation by R. Sterling and W. Scott. New York: Norton, 1985.

Supplementary Reading:

A mountain of secondary literature has been produced on the *Republic*. What follows below is a very small sample. Most of the books cited below are explicitly designed as introductions, and they should be consulted first.

Annas, Julia. *An Introduction to Plato's Republic.* Oxford: Oxford University Press, 1985. A difficult but excellent overview of the *Republic*.

Aristotle. *The Politics.* Translation by Carnes Lord. Chicago: University of Chicago Press, 1984. Book II of this work contains Aristotle's criticism of the *Republic*.

Augustine: *Confessions.* F.J. Sheed, trans. Indianapolis: Hackett, 1992. The spiritual autobiography of one of the great Christian philosophers, who was deeply influenced by Platonism.

Bloom, Allan. *The Closing of the American Mind.* New York: Basic Books, 1984. A Platonic critique of American society. Bloom's comments about what he takes to be the harmful effects of contemporary music are particularly interesting.

Campbell, Alastair. *Medical Ethics.* Oxford: Oxford University Press, 2001. A good overview of the field of medical ethics as it is practiced today.

Cropsey, Joseph, and Leo Strauss. eds. *History of Political Philosophy.* Chicago: University of Chicago Press, 2003 (3rd ed.). Contains long and helpful essays on Aristotle, Machiavelli, Hobbes, Kant, Mill, Marx, and others.

Dillon, John, ed. *The Greek Sophists.* New York: Penguin, 2003. The most recent collection of the remaining writings of the Greek Sophists. It should be consulted by anyone interested in the relativism of Thrasymachus.

Ferrari, G. *City and Soul in Plato's Republic.* Sankt Augustin: Academia Verlag, 2003. An interesting and comprehensive discussion of the city-soul analogy.

Fine, Gail, ed. *Plato.* Oxford: Oxford University Press, 2000. A massive book of nearly 1,000 pages that contains 37 articles that have been published on Plato. Virtually every subject is treated in this book.

Hammond, N., and H. Scullard, eds. *The Oxford Classical Dictionary.* Oxford: Clarendon Press, 1970. An authoritative reference work. It was used as the source for the biographical and historical material cited in this course.

Hesiod. *The Theogony.* There are many translations of this, one of the earliest Greek poems. It tells the story of the birth of the gods and is targeted for censorship by Socrates in Book II of the *Republic.*

Hobbes, Thomas. *Leviathan.* Originally published in 1651, this is one of the founding texts in the history of modern political philosophy.

Homer. *The Odyssey.* There are many translations of this, the foremost Greek epic. It is specifically targeted for censorship by Socrates in Book II of the *Republic.* It should be read as the paradigmatic poem in the "old quarrel between philosophy and poetry."

Honderich, Ted, ed. *The Oxford Companion to Philosophy.* Oxford: Oxford University Press, 1995. An excellent source book that contains clear, short introductions to basic philosophical concepts and figures.

Howland, Jacob. *The Republic: The Odyssey of Philosophy.* Philadelphia: Paul Dry, 2004. An excellent introduction to the dialogue that pays particular attention to its literary form. It also has a good glossary and timeline.

Huxley, Aldous. *Brave New World.* New York: Time Books, 1963. One of the greatest 20th-century dystopia novels. Some would argue that the just city of Plato's *Republic* is dystopic.

Kant, Immanuel. *Foundations of the Metaphysics of Morals.* Many translations are available of this work, first published in 1785 and one of the most influential works in the history of moral philosophy. Kant famously argues here that lying can never be morally justified.

Klein, Jacob. *A Commentary on Plato's Meno.* Chapel Hill, NC: University of North Carolina Press, 1965. This book contains (on pages 115–125) the best short explanation of the divided line that I have encountered.

Kraut, Richard, ed. *The Cambridge Companion to Plato.* Cambridge: Cambridge University Press, 1992. Contains 15 essays on Plato's thought. Some are difficult, but all were written for this volume, which is designed as an introduction to Platonic scholarship.

———, ed. *Plato's Republic: Critical Essays.* Lanham, MD: Rowman & Littlefield, 1997. A collection of 13 essays about the *Republic.* Several were cited in this course, including David Sachs, "A Fallacy in Plato's *Republic*"; Bernard Williams, "The Analogy of City and Soul in Plato's *Republic*"; Jonathan Lear, "Inside and Outside the *Republic*"; Iris Murdoch, "The Sovereignty of the Good"; Arlene Saxonhouse, "The Philosopher and the Female in the Political Thought of Plato"; Gregory Vlastos, "Was Plato a Feminist?"

Lane, Melissa. *Plato's Progeny: How Plato and Socrates Still Captivate the Modern Mind.* London: Duckworth, 2001. Designed for the general reader, this book gives a glimpse of Plato's influence on the modern world.

Machiavelli, Niccolo. *The Prince.* Written in 1513, this is, with Hobbes's *Leviathan*, generally considered to be a foundational text in the history of modern political philosophy. Thrasymachus's position on justice seems, at times, to foreshadow Machiavelli's views.

Marx, Karl. *The Communist Manifesto.* Written in 1848, this short work spells out some of the basic tenets of modern communism, a position perhaps foreshadowed in Books II–IV of Plato's *Republic.*

Mill, John Stuart. *Utilitarianism.* Written in 1863, this is Mill's classic explanation of the moral position of utilitarianism.

————. *On Liberty.* Written in 1859, this short book contains the classic defense of modern "liberalism."

Mitchell, B., and J. R. Lucas. *An Engagement with Plato's Republic: A Companion to the Republic.* London: Ashgate, 2003. A lucid introduction to some of the basic philosophical issues found in the dialogue.

Monoson, Sara. *Plato's Democratic Entanglements.* Princeton: Princeton University Press, 2000. This book defends the controversial thesis that Plato was not as hostile to democracy as is usually thought.

Orwell, George. *1984.* Oxford: Oxford University Press, 1984. One of the great 20th-century dystopia novels. Some would count Plato's *Republic* as a dystopia.

Plato: *Five Dialogues of Plato.* G.M.A. Grubem trans. Indianapolis: Hackett, 1982. Contains a good translation of the *Apology of Socrates*, which should be read as a companion to the *Republic*.

Popper, Karl. *The Open Society and Its Enemies.* Princeton: Princeton University Press, 1950. This famous book includes a scathing critique of Plato, whom Popper accuses of being an enemy of an open, progressive, freedom-loving society.

Press, G. *Who Speaks for Plato?* Lanham, MD: Rowman & Littlefield, 2000. A collection of 15 essays that address the question: Why did Plato write dialogues?

Roochnik, David. *Beautiful City: The Dialectical Character of Plato's Republic.* Ithaca: Cornell University Press, 2003. A difficult book aimed at Plato scholars. It presents an interpretation of the entire dialogue that takes its bearings from the idea of dialectic.

————. *Retrieving the Ancients: An Introduction to Greek Philosophy.* London: Blackwell, 2004. An overview of the history of Greek philosophy; designed for introductory students.

Samons, Loren. *What's Wrong with Democracy? From Athenian Practice to American Worship.* Berkeley: University of California Press, 2004. A controversial book that sketches the history of Athenian democracy and offers a sharp critique of the contemporary understanding of it.

Strauss, Leo. *The City and Man.* Chicago: University of Chicago Press, 1974. A controversial book that argues that Plato is essentially an ironic writer.

Vlastos, Gregory, ed. *Plato I: Metaphysics and Epistemology.* New York: Anchor Books, 1971. A collection of 13 essays on Plato's metaphysics and epistemology. Some are too technical for the general reader, but the first three are useful as introductions to Plato's theory of Ideas.